Better Homes and Gardens®

CHERISHED

D·O·L·L·S

TO MAKE FOR FUN

© Copyright 1984 by Meredith Corporation, Des Moines, Iowa.
All Rights Reserved. Printed in the United States of America.
First Edition. Sixth Printing, 1985.
Library of Congress Catalog Card Number: 80-68542
ISBN: 0-696-01075-5 (hard cover)
ISBN: 0-696-01077-1 (trade paperback)

# BETTER HOMES AND GARDENS® BOOKS

Editor: Gerald M. Knox
Art Director: Ernest Shelton
Managing Editor: David A. Kirchner

Crafts Editor: Nancy Lindemeyer
Senior Crafts Books Editor: Joan Cravens
Associate Crafts Books Editors: Debra Felton,
    Laura Holtorf, James A. Williams

Associate Art Directors: Linda Ford, Neoma Alt West,
    Randall Yontz
Copy and Production Editors: Marsha Jahns,
    Nancy Nowiszewski, Mary Helen Schiltz,
    David A. Walsh
Assistant Art Directors: Harijs Priekulis, Tom Wegner
Senior Graphic Designers: Alisann Dixon, Lynda Haupert,
    Lyne Neymeyer
Graphic Designers: Mike Burns, Mike Eagleton,
    Deb Miner, Stan Sams, D. Greg Thompson,
    Darla Whipple, Paul Zimmerman

Editor in Chief: Neil Kuehnl
Group Editorial Services Director: Duane L. Gregg

General Manager: Fred Stines
Director of Publishing: Robert B. Nelson
Director of Retail Marketing: Jamie Martin
Director of Direct Marketing: Arthur Heydendael


**Cherished Dolls to Make for Fun**
Crafts Editor: Laura Holtorf
Copy and Production Editor: Nancy Nowiszewski
Graphic Designer: Alisann Dixon

# C·O·N·T·E·N·T·S

# DOLL-MAKER'S WORKSHOP
## —THE ART OF THE CRAFT

What a magical craft doll making is! With fabrics, yarn braids or curls, and a perfectly stitched smile, you can bring to life a new friend. To illustrate the versatility of the craft, this book begins with a special section featuring these three dolls—all made from one basic pattern (instructions begin on page 6).

In the chapters following, you'll find dozens of dolls for children to play with and for you to use and display in your home. The dolls are crafted of fabric, yarn, clay, and wood, plus plenty of imagination. You will also find expert tips on everything from doll dressing to stuffing tiny fingers and toes. In all, this book offers an extraordinary collection of dolls, with extra details to help make each doll truly your own.

## BASIC DOLL BODY

Imagination and a basic pattern are all you need to create dolls in several styles. The three dolls shown on pages 4 and 5 are a case in point: Each is made from the same body pattern, but each doll has its own distinct look and personality.

The directions for adapting and stitching a basic pattern are included below. You'll find specific instructions for each doll, along with full-size face patterns, on the following pages.

### Materials
*(for doll body)*
(Yardage is 45 inches wide.)
- ½ yard of body fabric (white fabric for Victorian lady, muslin for country girl, and pink fabric for boy doll)
- ½ yard of striped fabric (country girl legs)
- Polyester fiberfill; thread

### Instructions
Enlarge body, leg, and arm patterns, *right,* onto brown paper. Add ¼ inch for seam allowances except as noted below.

Use the pattern "as is" for the Victorian lady. For the country girl, shorten the arm by 2½ inches. For the blue-jeaned pal, do not add seam allowances (this narrows the entire body); shorten the arm by 2½ inches and the leg by 1½ inches.

Cut out paper patterns; position them on fabrics noted in the materials list. Trace body pattern onto fabric, but *do not cut out body piece until face is complete.*

For Victorian and country dolls, transfer the face to one body piece by placing fabric over the face pattern and tracing the features with a water-erasable marking pen. For the boy doll, see instructions on page 11.

Work faces according to the instructions for the individual dolls. When faces are complete, cut out the body pieces.

To assemble dolls, sew pattern pieces together with right sides facing, unless otherwise noted in the instructions for each doll. To begin, stitch body pieces together, leaving openings at the armholes and at the bottom; turn.

Sew arm pattern pieces together, leaving tops open. Clip curves, trim seams, turn, and stuff. Sew opening closed. Insert arms into body; sew in place.

Repeat the process, *above,* for legs (toes should point up).

Finally, dress your doll following instructions for the individual dolls and referring to pages 46 and 47 for ideas for doll clothes.

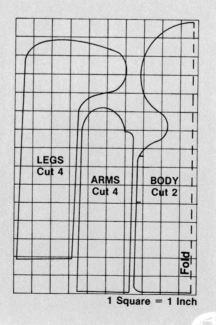

LEGS
Cut 4

ARMS
Cut 4

BODY
Cut 2

Fold

**1 Square = 1 Inch**

**I**nspired by Victorian elegance, we've dressed this collectible doll in emerald satin with flourishes of laces and ribbons that are true to turn-of-the-century style.

### Materials
(Yardage is for 45-inch-wide fabric.)
- 1¼ yards of green taffeta (dress)
- 4½ yards of ⅝-inch-wide blue satin picot-trim ribbon (ruching and bouquet ribbon on skirt)
- 1 yard of ½-inch-wide patterned ribbon (collar, cuff, bodice trim)
- ½ yard of 2-inch-wide lace (bodice ruffle)
- 12 inches of 1¼-inch-wide eyelet (belt)
- 18 inches of ⅜-inch-wide yellow satin (belt, collar bow)
- 12 small pearl beads (buttons)
- 1 purple glass button (collar trim)
- 1 yard of white fabric (pantaloons and slip)
- 1½ yards of ¼-inch-wide yellow ribbon
- 2¼ yards of 2-inch-wide preruffled white eyelet (pantaloon and slip trim)
- ⅛ yard of black satin (shoes)
- 14 small pearl buttons (shoe buttons)
- Assorted artificial flowers
- 1 yard of ⅛-inch-wide blue satin ribbon (hair bows)
- 1 skein of brown yarn (hair)
- Black, white, and rose embroidery floss
- Water-erasable marking pen
- Graph paper
- Embroidery hoop and needle

## Instructions

Assemble the doll following the general instructions, *opposite.*

**To embroider face:** Satin-stitch the mouth with pink floss and the pupils and nostrils with black floss. Outline-stitch the eyelashes, eyebrows, and eyelids with black. Add white French knots to highlight the eyes.

**Hair:** Cut yarn into 36-inch lengths. Cut a 1x4-inch strip from muslin. Center yarn along strip, covering the entire length. Stitch down the center of the strip (this becomes the part). Whipstitch part to head.

*Note:* Before making curls, cover embroidered face with plastic wrap to keep it clean. Curls are positioned in a thick, continuous row of curls from one side of the head, around the back, to the opposite side of the head.

For each curl, separate six strands of yarn. Spray yarn lightly with hair spray. Wrap the yarn around a thick pencil (¾-inch diameter). Then, carefully slip the curl from the pencil into position on the head. Loop matching color thread through curl and tie a knot to the underside. Tack curl to head. *Note:* Stitch curls to the hair, instead of to the head, as you build up layers of curls. Continue making curls until all of the yarn is used or until you achieve the desired effect. Add narrow ribbon bows and artificial flowers.

**Clothing: To make the high-button shoes:** Using the original leg/foot pattern, trace the shoe shape onto tissue paper ⅛ inch beyond the original seam lines so that it measures 6 inches from the sole to the cuff. Cut two pairs of shoe shapes from black satin.

*Note:* Stitch the pattern pieces together with right sides facing, unless otherwise noted.

Stitch shoes together, leaving the back seam open for fitting. Trim the seams, clip curves, and turn; press.

Slip the shoes onto the feet, turn raw edges of back seam under, and slip-stitch closed. Turn under raw edges at the top of the shoes and slip-stitch boots to legs at cuff.

Stitch seven small pearl buttons along center front seam of each shoe, spacing buttons evenly from mid-toe to top of shoe.

**Pantaloons:** Refer to the boy doll jeans pattern on page 13 to create the pantaloons pattern. Draw a parallel line 1½ inches from the fold line. This becomes the fold line for the pantaloons pattern. Cut two pattern pieces from white fabric.

Stitch each leg along the inseams; stitch legs together.

Turn under the top edge of pantaloons ½ inch, insert a strip of narrow elastic, and stitch the seam down, leaving an opening at the back seam. Stitch the ends of the elastic together to make a 7-inch circle; slip-stitch the opening closed. Trim pantaloons legs just above the shoe cuff; hand-stitch eyelet and ribbon to bottom of each leg. Place pantaloons on doll.

**Slip:** Cut a 4x12-inch rectangle from white fabric for the yoke of the slip. Make casing as directed *above* for pantaloons. Cut a 6x36-inch strip of white fabric. Border one long strip edge with 2-inch-wide pregathered eyelet trim, woven with narrow yellow ribbon. Stitch short ends of strip together; press seams. Gather the top edge of fabric; adjust gathers to fit yoke bottom; stitch together.

**Dress:** *For the skirt:* Cut 9x36-inch rectangle from green tafetta. Border skirt with 5-inch-wide ruffle of taffeta; hem the ruffle. Gather the waist to fit, and add a narrow waistband to the skirt. Run a gathering thread through the center of blue satin picot ribbon;

pull the gathers; trim the skirt/ruffle seam with gathered ribbon to simulate old-fashioned ruching.

*For blouse:* Cut a 6x12-inch rectangle from green taffeta. Fold in half along the width, creating blouse front and back. Cut up the middle of the back half for back opening; cut small circle along fold for the neck opening. Hem the back opening; bind the neck opening with a 1-inch-wide bias-cut taffeta strip for a high collar.

*For sleeves:* Cut two 8x13-inch taffeta rectangles; stitch short sides together. Gather one end on each of the sleeves to fit the wrists.

Stitch a 1-inch-wide wristband to each sleeve; fold under ½ inch and slip-stitch in place. Gather the other end of the sleeves to 6 inches to fit at shoulders. Stitch the bodice seams; hand-stitch sleeves in place.

Trim sleeves with bands of gathered picot ribbon (refer to photo), and add narrow bands of patterned ribbon at collar and cuffs.

*For yoke:* Gather lace for bodice ruffle; slip-stitch gathered edges together, forming yoke. Stitch patterned ribbon over seam, forming a point at the bottom of the ribbon. Stitch the yoke to the bodice and trim with tiny seed-pearl buttons.

Add lace and bows at neck and waist; trim throat with glass button "brooch." Add bouquet of ribbons and flowers at hem.

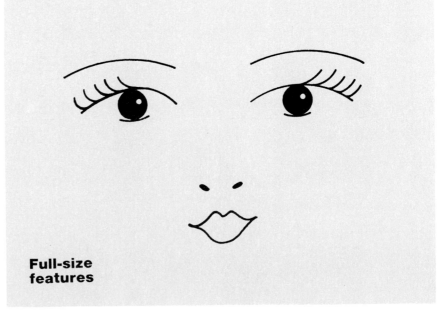

**Full-size features**

# C·O·U·N·T·R·Y    G·I·R·L

**F**rom her stockinged legs to her braided hair, this doll is a treasure of country-style trims and materials. She's easy to stitch, too. Make just one simple change in the basic pattern, and sew her up according to the instructions on page 6.

Follow directions here and on page 10 for her face, dress, and pinafore. Then add a straw hat for a country touch. And if you knit or crochet, you may wish to create a soft shawl from scraps of knitting worsted yarn in colors that complement her Sunday-best country clothes.

## Materials

- ⅔ yard of green plaid fabric (dress)
- ⅔ yard of tiny floral print fabric (apron)
- ⅔ yard of muslin (slip, panties)
- 1½ yards of 3½-inch-wide white lace (collar, sleeve trim)
- ⅓ yard of narrow white lace trim (collar)
- 1 yard each of ½-inch-wide ecru lace and eyelet trims
- 8x12 inches of brown felt (shoes)
- Two ¾-inch-diameter brown wooden buttons (shoes)
- 5 small ecru buttons
- 1 skein of Tahki's Doneghal Tweed brown yarn (hair)
- 1 yard of ⅝-inch-wide blue-green satin ribbon
- Embroidery hoop
- Embroidery needle
- Green, pink, white, and brown embroidery floss
- 1 yard of ⅛-inch-wide ecru lace (optional)
- Purchased straw hat (optional)
- Tiny green earring or glass bead (brooch)
- Brown paper

## Instructions

Make the doll following the basic doll pattern on page 6. *Note:* Be sure to cut the leg patterns from striped fabric for the stocking effect.

**Face:** Using three strands of embroidery floss, satin-stitch the eyes with green, the eyelashes with brown, and the mouth with pink (fill in the lower lip with satin stitches as shown in the photograph, if desired). Highlight the eyes with small, white straight stitches. Back-stitch all of the remaining lines with brown floss. Brush the cheeks with powdered rouge.

**Hair:** Open skein of yarn; cut the strands at one end and lay yarn out flat. Remove two strands to use for bangs and set them aside.

Cut a 3x6-inch wig strip from muslin. Locate the center of the yarn lengths. Center the yarn along the 6-inch wig strip; machine-stitch the yarn to the muslin strip.

*For bangs:* Clip approximately thirty 2-inch strands of yarn from the two yarn strands that were set aside. Position the strands side by side and lay a 5-inch strip of adhesive tape across the top of the strands. Then, machine-stitch across the yarn and tape.

Position the wig approximately 1 inch below the seam line at the center front of the head. Slip the bangs beneath the wig.

Slip-stitch the bangs and the wig to the head. Trim bangs.

Braid the yarn on either side of the head to the desired length; trim away excess yarn, and secure the braids. Tie braids with blue-green ribbons. Secure braids to base of head.

**Clothing:** Enlarge pattern pieces on page 10 onto brown paper. Add ½
*(continued)*

**Full-size features**

## Country Girl

*(continued)*

inch for all clothing seam allowances. Add a ¼-inch seam allowance to the shoes. Cut out pattern pieces.

**For shoes:** Cut four shoe pieces and four straps from brown felt.

Stitch the strap pieces together (in pairs), leaving an opening for turning. Clip curves, turn to the right side, and press. Topstitch close to the edge.

Stitch the shoes together (in pairs), from the heel to the toe area. Turn under raw edges at the top of the shoe and topstitch by machine or by hand. Place shoes on doll.

Slip straps under shoe on the inner side of each shoe; slip-stitch straps in place. Tack the curved edge of strap to outside of shoe.

Sew large brown buttons atop the curved strap edge.

**Panties:** Make panties from ecru fabric, following instructions given for the Victorian lady.

*Note:* Adjust the pantaloon leg length to make short briefs.

**Slip:** Using the pinafore pattern, cut the slip front and back on the fold, from muslin, adding 2 inches to the hem for extra length.

Stitch the front to the back at sides and shoulders. Clip the armhole and neck seam allowances; press under ½ inch and topstitch in place. Trim with ⅛-inch-wide ecru lace.

Do not hem the slip until the dress is completed. Place slip on doll.

**Dress:** Cut dress front and back, and a 2x4½-inch rectangle (facing for back opening) from green plaid fabric. Mark a 3½-inch slit starting from center back neck.

With right sides facing, center the rectangle over the slit; carefully stitch ¼ inch around slit marking, bringing stitching to a point at slit bottom.

Cut slit through both layers. Turn facing to inside; slip-stitch in place.

Stitch the front to the back at the shoulders, sleeves, and side seams. Clip neck edge; turn under ½ inch and topstitch close to edge.

Place dress on doll over slip. Turn under ½ inch twice on bottom dress edge and hem. Turn under bottom edge of slip so that it peeks ½ inch

from under the dress hem. Stitch ½-inch-wide eyelet trim to bottom of slip and a row of lace just above eyelet trim. Catch the hem as trims are stitched in place.

Turn under hem on sleeves, allowing 1 inch for placement of lace trim. Place lace under the sleeve and catch hem as trim is stitched to sleeve.

**Collar:** *Note:* The collar is a separate piece, and is *not* attached to the neck of the dress.

Run a gathering stitch along one long edge of the 3½-inch-wide lace. Pull gathers of lace collar to fit around dress neck edge and secure thread. Or, pull gathers up tight, so collar fits securely around neck (as pictured). Stitch a row of white narrow lace over gathering thread. Turn under short sides and hem. Place collar on doll and fasten in back. Trim collar front with a tiny earring "brooch."

**Pinafore:** From tiny floral print fabric, cut the back piece on the fold, cut two front pieces on the selvage, and one 2-inch-square pocket.

Cut lining fronts and a back, using the pinafore pattern.

Stitch pinafore fronts to back at shoulders and sides. Repeat for lining. Stitch lining to pinafore at fronts, and around neck and bottom edges. Do not stitch around the armholes. Turn to right side, clip curves, and press. Clip the armhole seam allowances; press under ½ inch on lining and pinafore and slip-stitch together. Work five tiny buttonholes, evenly spaced, on the right side of the pinafore. (For best results, work buttonhole stitches by hand.) Stitch buttons onto the left side. Or, fasten the pinafore using snaps, and sew buttons to the right side of the pinafore.

*For pocket:* Turn under ¼ inch on all sides. Slip-stitch lace across the top edge. Sew pocket to pinafore.

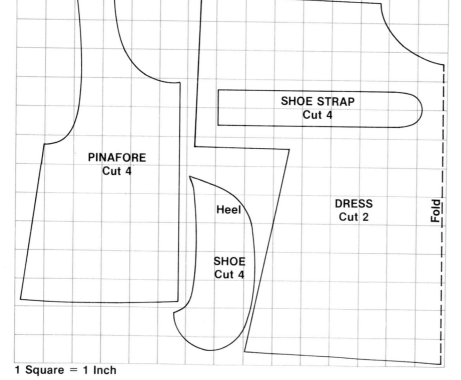

**1 Square = 1 Inch**

# B·L·U·E-J·E·A·N·E·D  P·A·L

**A** clever change of fabric, clothing, and facial features is all it takes to turn our basic doll pattern into this rugged outdoorsman.

Give this young fellow lots of personality by adding ears to his head, trapunto quilting his pug nose, and using red yarn for his close-cropped hair.

For the body pattern and sewing directions, turn to page 6. Specific instructions and the full-size face pattern begin on page 12.

*(continued)*

## Blue-Jeaned Pal

*(continued)*

Assemble the boy doll following the basic doll body instructions found on page 6.

### Materials

- ¼ yard of quilted fabric (vest)
- ¼ yard of plaid cotton fabric (shirt)
- ⅓ yard of denim fabric (jeans)
- 9x12 inches of brown felt (shoes)
- Scraps of blue and white felt (eyes)
- 20 yards of orange yarn (hair)
- Red embroidery floss (mouth)
- 12 inches of narrow elastic
- 7-inch square of nonwoven interfacing
- Medium-weight 14-inch-long separating zipper
- Powdered rouge
- Matching thread
- White glue

### Instructions

Assemble the boy doll following the basic doll body instructions found on page 6.

**Face:** Trace full-size face pattern, *below,* in place onto body pattern, using a water-erasable marking pen.

Lay lightweight interfacing over the pattern; using a pencil, trace around the head outline and the nose and mouth features. Mark dots for placement of eyes.

Lay the marked interfacing on the wrong side of one body piece; machine-stitch over the penciled lines using white thread. Mark the eyes with knotted thread.

*To pad the nose:* Cut a horizontal slit in the interfacing between the stitching. Stuff a small amount of polyester fiberfill into the opening. Pull the slit together with overcast stitches.

Embroider mouth with split stitches, using three strands of red embroidery floss. Embroider stitches directly over the white guideline.

Cut two white felt circles for the eyes. Glue in place. Cut two smaller blue felt circles; glue in place. Color the cheeks with powdered rouge.

*For ears:* Cut two 1½-inch-diameter circles from pink fabric, and add ¼-inch seam allowances. Cut circles in half. Stitch the halves together along the curved edge. Turn to the right side and stuff with fiberfill. Position ears so that they face inward toward face; baste in place.

**Shoes:** Following the foot/leg pattern, trace the shoe shape onto tissue paper ⅛ inch outside the original seam lines and measuring approximately 3½ inches high. Cut two pairs of shoe shapes from brown felt.

Stitch the shoes together (in pairs) with right sides facing, leaving the back seam open for fitting. Trim the seams, clip curves, turn, and press.

Slip the shoes onto the feet, turn raw edges of back seam under, and slip-stitch closed. Slip-stitch boots to legs at boot top.

**Hair:** Cut two 4½-yard lengths and two 5½-yard lengths from orange yarn. Wind one of the 5½-yard lengths around a 2x7-inch piece of cardboard, widthwise. Using a zipper foot, machine-stitch down one side of the cardboard to hold the strands together. Slip yarn off the cardboard. Repeat for second 5½-yard length.

Hand-stitch one group of loops to the head between the ears, placing the loose loops along bottom hairline; slip-stitch the loops to the hairline.

Layer a second group of loops atop the first, placing one short end just in front of the ear, curving the layer to the opposite side in front of the other ear; stitch in place. Slip-stitch loops to the first layer.

Wind one 4½-yard length lengthwise around a 3x4½-inch piece of cardboard. Machine-stitch down one side of the cardboard for 2 inches. Slip yarn from cardboard. Repeat for the second length.

Layer these groups across the top of the head, following the hairline guide and creating a part on the left

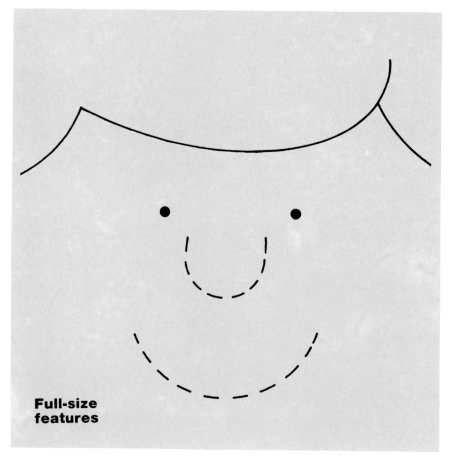

**Full-size features**

side. Hand-stitch in place, forming curls and swirls of hair.

**Clothing:** Enlarge patterns, *at right,* onto tissue paper, adding ¼ inch for seam allowances; cut out.

**For the shirt:** Cut the pattern pieces and two 2½x5½-inch pieces (cuffs) from plaid fabric.

Stitch the fronts to the back at the shoulder seams.

Fold the collar lengthwise; stitch short ends together. Turn and press. Match center back neck to center collar. Baste in place, folding shirt facings outside over the collar. Stitch through all thicknesses. Turn facings to the inside and press fronts. Topstitch collar and fronts.

Match center of sleeves to the shirt shoulder seams; stitch in place. Sew cuffs to the sleeves. Press cuff in half to the inside; topstitch. Stitch sleeve and side seams. Hem the shirttail. Work four buttonholes along left shirt front. Sew buttons on right side. Or, fasten with four snaps and sew buttons on top of left front.

**Pants:** *Note:* Use white thread for topstitching throughout.

Cut jeans and two front pockets from blue denim fabric.

Press under hem allowance on pockets; topstitch the slanted "openings." Place the pockets on the front of the pants where marked on pattern; topstitch in place.

Topstitch a hem across the bottom of each pant leg. Stitch the center front seams and topstitch a mock fly opening. Stitch center back seams. Stitch the front and back inner leg seams. Press under the waistline hem and topstitch. Stitch the ends of 12-inch-long elastic together, making a circle. Place under hem inside the waist. Stitch the hem down, enclosing the elastic. (Pull the fabric taut when stitching, to form "boxer" top.)

**Vest:** Cut the vest, using shirt front and back patterns (omitting the facings) from quilted fabric. Cut pockets, using pants-pocket pattern.

Hem slanted pocket edge. Baste under top edge and long side. Place pocket on vest front, even with the side and bottom edges. Topstitch in place. Repeat for other pocket.

Stitch the side seams, catching pockets in stitching. Hem the sleeve openings, fronts, and bottom edge.

Position the separating zipper, with teeth showing, having bottom even with jacket bottom. *Note:* Trim top of zipper to fit vest. Baste and stitch in place. Trim bottom zipper edge and overcast edge.

Cut 1x6-inch length of quilted fabric to bind neckline. Separate fabric and use only one strip. Stitch strip to neckline and top of zipper. Fold over, forming a collar band; slip-stitch in place.

**Accessories:** Cut a scarf from red plaid wool fabric and fringe the ends. Make cap as directed for the baseball dolls on page 57.

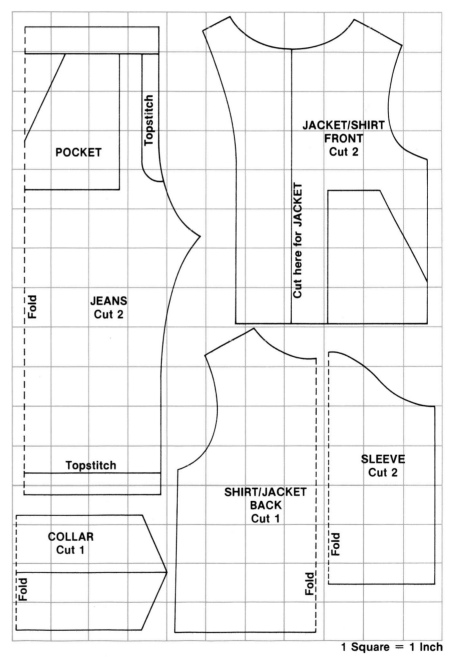

1 Square = 1 Inch

# PLAYTIME PALS

Huggable, fanciful, and a child's best friend—that's what a doll should be. From the delightful schoolgirl shown here to the lovable playmates on the next few pages, your child is sure to find the ideal pal. The instructions for this doll begin on the next page. For tips on making her wardrobe, see pages 46 to 49.

# B·E·S·T - F·R·I·E·N·D   D·O·L·L

**J**ust like a brand-new playmate come to stay, the charming schoolgirl shown on pages 14 and 15 is a perfect make-believe companion. She stands just 13 inches tall, but her embroidered face, crimped red hair, and detailed arms and legs make her life-like enough for a little girl to dress in style. You can stitch an entire wardrobe of clothes tailored just for her, or dress her in miniature versions of your daughter's clothes. For specific doll-dressing and doll-making tips, see the special section on pages 46 to 49.

## Materials

### Body
- ⅓ yard of 45-inch-wide flesh-colored, firmly woven cotton
- 1 skein of nubby red yarn (hair)
- Brown and red embroidery floss (face)
- Polyester fiberfill
- Small scraps of white and brown bonded mending tape (eyes)

### Clothing

#### Camisole and panty
- 28 inches of 3½-inch-wide white embroidered eyelet
- 22 inches of matching ½-inch-wide white embroidered eyelet
- 1 yard of ⅛-inch-wide light blue satin ribbon
- 9 inches of round elastic
- 2 small snaps

#### Stockings
- 4x12 inches of white fine-knit fabric (or piece cut from child's stocking)

#### Shoes
- 10x14 inches of black satin
- 10-inch-square of medium-weight iron-on interfacing
- 3x4 inches of black bonded mending tape
- 3x4 inches of fusible webbing
- 3½x6 inches of gray fabric

#### Dress
- ¼ yard of 45-inch-wide baby blue pinstripe fabric
- 9 inches of ⅛-inch-wide royal blue satin ribbon
- 2 small white buttons
- 1 hook-and-eye fastener
- Scrap of bias tape

#### Collar
- 6x12 inches *each* of white fabric and interfacing
- 20 inches of ⅛-inch-wide royal blue satin ribbon
- 1 hook-and-eye fastener
- 14 inches of ⅝-inch-wide red satin ribbon (tie)

#### Purse
- 9x12 inches of red fabric
- Scrap of white bonded mending tape (star)
- 1 small snap

### Hat
- Purchased white straw hat
- ⅜-inch-wide royal blue satin ribbon equal to circumference of crown plus 1 inch
- 32 inches of ⅞-inch-wide royal blue satin ribbon

## Instructions
Finished size is 13 inches high.

*Note:* Before you begin, refer to pages 48 and 49 for special tips for making and dressing a perfect doll.

Enlarge the patterns, *opposite,* onto brown paper; cut out pattern pieces. Patterns include ¼-inch seam allowances, unless noted *below.*

**Body:** Cut two body pieces from flesh-colored fabric. Stitch pieces together, right sides facing, leaving an opening for turning at the neck edge. (Use 15 to 20 stitches per inch for machine stitching.) Double-stitch all of the seams for sturdiness. Clip curves, turn to the right side, and stuff firmly with fiberfill. *Note:* See page 23 for tips on stuffing dolls.

Slip-stitch the opening closed.

**Legs:** Cut four leg patterns from flesh-colored fabric. Patterns include ⅛-inch seam allowances for *center front and back seams only.* Otherwise, use ¼-inch seam allowances. Stitch legs together, right sides facing; make two. Leave base and top of each leg open. Trim; clip curves.

Cut out two soles from flesh-colored fabric. With right sides facing, stitch soles to base of legs. Clip curves, turn, and stuff legs firmly. Slip-stitch opening closed and whipstitch legs to body.

**Arms:** Cut four arms from flesh-colored fabric. Patterns include ⅛-inch seam allowances.

With right sides facing, stitch arms together; make two. Leave an opening at the top of each arm.

Stitch the fingers very carefully. Trim seam allowance of the fingers close to the stitching and carefully clip between the fingers.

*(continued)*

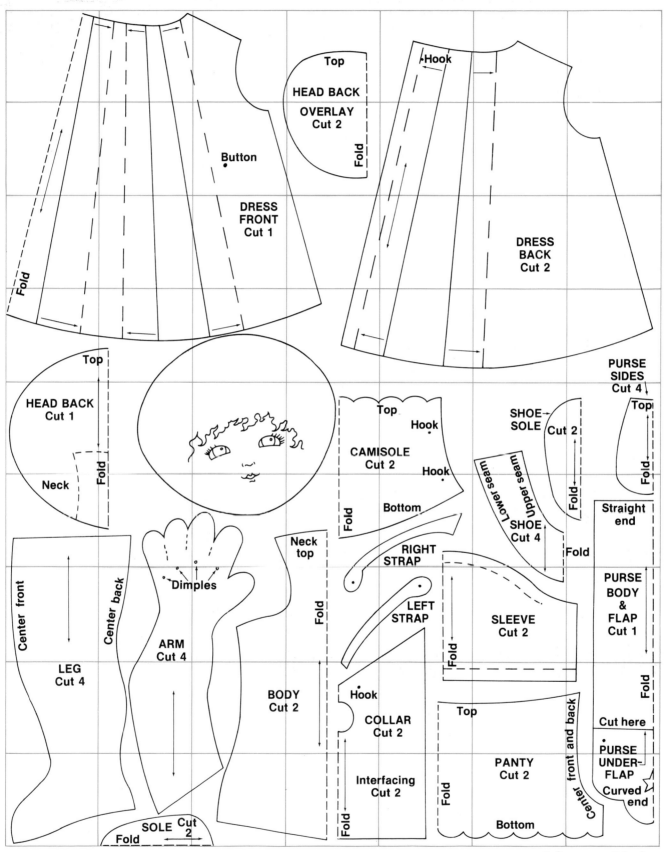

1 Square = 2 Inches

## Best-Friend Doll
### (continued)

**Full-size features**

Use a small blunt object to turn and stuff the fingers. Place a tiny amount of fiberfill into each fingertip.

Stuff hands moderately and evenly; insert a pin across each wrist to hold stuffing in place.

Bend hands into a natural curve; secure bends with pins, and adjust stuffing if needed. Sew small tucks in the palm of the left hand to shape, if desired. On right hand, tack fingers into a bent position. Remove the pins and continue stuffing. On the right arm, stop stuffing at the elbow; bend and secure with pins. Blindstitch bend on the back of the arm.

Finish stuffing the arm. Turn the tops of the arms to the inside and slip-stitch arm tops closed.

Use sewing thread to define the fingers and stitch the dimples. Slip-stitch the arms to the body.

**Face:** Trace the full-size facial features, *above,* onto tissue paper.

Trace the outline of one head pattern onto flesh-colored fabric. Transfer the face to the head front, using dressmaker's carbon. Do not cut out.

Cut the eyes from white bonded mending tape. Bond eyes to face following the manufacturer's directions. Add brown mending tape for pupils.

**Embroidered facial details:** With one strand of sewing thread, outline the eyes using brown backstitches; embroider straight stitches for the eyelashes, white French knots for eye accents, and burgundy satin stitches for the mouth and nose.

Lightly brush the cheeks with powdered rouge.

**Head:** *Note:* The head and overlay are two separate units. The back of the head is stitched to the front of the neck, then the overlay is stitched over the neck and the back of the head for reinforcement.

Cut two overlays and two heads (one of the heads is the embroidered head pattern piece) from the flesh-colored fabric.

With right sides facing, stitch head front to back, leaving the top of the head open. Restitch and form a slightly rounded chin, if desired. Clip the curves, turn, and stuff firmly. Slip-stitch opening closed.

Stitch overlay pieces together, right sides facing, leaving an opening at the top. Cut out overlay, clip curves, and turn. Slip-stitch opening closed.

To attach head to body, pin neck to back of head, using the dashed lines on the back head pattern as a guide; stitch in place.

Pin overlay to the back of the head and over the neck, using the dotted lines on the pattern as a guide. Stitch the overlay to the head along the outer edges.

**Hair:** Wrap yarn about 100 times around the width of a 5x10-inch piece of cardboard. Cut yarn along one side of the cardboard.

Cut a 2x6-inch strip from muslin. Center the yarn strands along the width of the strip, and machine-stitch down the middle. Clip the muslin strip close to the stitching line.

Fold yarn in half with muslin on the inside; pin wig to seam line around the face. Pull several strands from the wig to form bangs and frame the face.

Trim yarn and stitch to the face. Slip-stitch the wig to the head along the seam line; clip hair.

**Clothing: Camisole:** Cut the patterns from eyelet, placing the scalloped edge of the eyelet at the top edge of the camisole.

Lace pale blue ribbon through the eyelet scallops. Tie and stitch a narrow ribbon bow to the center top of the camisole front.

Stitch one side seam. For remaining edges, press seam allowances under; topstitch. Sew two hook-and-eye fasteners to the sides.

To make straps for the camisole, cut narrow pale blue ribbon to size; tack the ends in place.

**Panty:** Cut two patterns from eyelet. Lace ribbon through the legs.

Stitch together the center front and back seams; clip curves.

To make waistline casing, press under ¼ inch along the top raw edge twice, hiding the raw edges. Stitch along the bottom edge, leaving an opening in the back through which to insert the elastic. Pull a length of elastic through the casing and secure; stitch the casing closed.

With right sides facing, stitch inner leg seams together.

**Stockings:** Wrap white knit fabric around the doll's foot, pulling fabric taut to the back and bottom of foot.

Pin along the back and bottom, creating a seam line. Remove fabric from the doll's foot.

Stitch along the pinned seam line. Trim the seams, clip the curves, and turn the stockings to the right side. Hem the top edge of the stockings.

**Shoes:** Cut four shoes from black satin fabric. Cut two sole pieces from gray fabric. Fuse together the wrong side of each shoe and sole piece with iron-on interfacing.

With right sides facing, pin two shoe pieces together along the upper seam line; stitch together. Clip curves.

With right sides facing, stitch the center back shoe seam; turn right side out and press. Stitch lower shoe edges together.

With right sides facing, pin one sole to each shoe; stitch together and clip curves. Turn to the right side.

To make shoe straps, cut straps from black bonded mending tape.

Fuse two 3x4-inch pieces of black satin fabric together with fusible webbing. Bond each strap to the fused fabric so that the finished straps are three layers thick.

Cut each strap and stitch to the sides of the shoes.

**Dress:** Transfer pleat lines to the wrong side of dress front and backs using dressmaker's carbon paper.

Cut one dress front, two backs, two sleeves, and one 2¼x7¾-inch rectangle (belt) from baby blue pinstripe fabric. Cut two 1½x4½-inch sleeve bands from white fabric.

To form pleats, bring solid lines to the dashed lines. Pin the front side pleats partially over the center pleat. Machine-baste front and back pleats together at neckline; press.

With right sides facing, stitch front to back at the shoulders. Stitch ⅛ inch from the neck edge; clip curves.

Matching raw edges, pin and stitch bias tape to right side of neck edge, easing to fit and having the bias ends extending ¼ inch past the back neck edge. Turn the tape to the inside; stitch it to the dress.

For sleeve bands, stitch narrow ribbon ½ inch from the edge of one long side on each band. Press under ¼ inch on one long side of each band.

Gather the tops and bottoms of the sleeves. With right sides facing, stitch a band to each sleeve, adjusting gathers to fit. Ease the top sleeve gathers to fit the sleeve opening.

With right sides facing, stitch sleeve to sleeve opening.

With right sides facing, stitch dress front to backs at sides and sleeves.

Turn the raw edge of the sleeve band to the inside of each sleeve; slip-stitch in place.

With right sides facing, pin dress together at center back and stitch a 2-inch-long seam starting from the bottom. Sew a hook-and-eye fastener at top of neck edge. Hem dress.

**Belt:** With right sides facing, fold the belt piece in half lengthwise and stitch raw edges together, rounding off the ends of the belt and leaving an opening for turning. Clip the curves, and turn belt to right side. Slip-stitch the opening closed.

Sew a buttonhole at each end of the belt. Sew the buttons to the sides of the dress. Button belt to dress.

**Collar:** Cut two collars from white fabric; cut two interfacings.

Stitch narrow blue ribbon to the right side of one collar ½ inch from each of the three straight sides.

Baste interfacing to the wrong side of each collar.

With right sides facing, stitch collars together, leaving an opening for turning. Clip curves, turn to right side, and slip-stitch opening closed. Attach hook-and-eye closure.

Cut points at the ends of red ribbon; tack the center of the ribbon to the back neckline of the dress.

Wrap the collar around the doll's neck, fastening it in the front. Bring the ribbon under the collar to the front of the dress; knot.

**Purse:** Cut out all purse patterns and one 1¼x9-inch handle from red fabric. Cut 1x2-inch piece of cardboard, and one star from a scrap of white bonded mending tape.

Bond star to purse. Press under ¼ inch along the straight ends of the purse and underflap; topstitch.

With right sides facing, stitch the underflap to the purse along curved edges. Clip curves; turn.

With right sides facing, stitch side pieces together (in pairs) along the top; turn to right side. Stitch each pair together along curved edges.

With right sides facing, stitch side pieces to purse, matching the top of each side piece to the straight end of the purse. Turn to the right side.

Insert cardboard piece into the bottom of the purse.

Press under ¼ inch on both long sides of the handle piece. Fold the handle in half lenthwise, with wrong sides facing. Topstitch close to the pressed edges and along the center of the handle.

Place ½ inch of the ends of the handle inside purse at sides; stitch in place. Sew a snap to the underside of the flap and purse.

**Hat:** Turn under ½ inch of narrow ribbon on one end. Tack ribbon to bottom of hat crown.

Tie wide ribbon into a bow; stitch toward hat back. Trim ribbon ends with an inverted V-cut.

# A·P·P·L·I·Q·U·É·D   C·H·A·R·A·C·T·E·R·S

**W**ho would guess that these Wild West cowboys and prima ballerinas were created from the same basic pattern? The construction just couldn't be simpler — stitch and stuff the fabric bodies, then create the characters by appliquéing denim jeans and a western-style shirt, or a leotard of tulle and satin.

## Materials for one ballerina

- ¼ yard of neutral-color fabric (body)
- ¼ yard of blue satin (leotard)
- 14x36 inches of blue tulle (tutu)
- Pearls (necklace)
- 10 inches of sequin trim
- 24 inches of ¼-inch-wide blue satin ribbon
- Blue and pink acrylic paints
- Black fine-point permanent marker
- Forty 30-inch strands of brown yarn
- Polyester fiberfill

## Materials for one cowboy

- ¼ yard of muslin (body)
- Fabric scraps (shirt, yokes, jeans)
- ¼ yard of suedecloth (hat, gloves, and boots)
- 8x12 inches of gingham (scarf)
- 1½ yards of fine cord (lasso)
- 2½ inches of ⅜-inch-wide white grosgrain ribbon (shirt placket)
- 12 inches of 1-inch-long fringe (shirt)
- Four ⅜-inch buttons (shirt)
- 10 inches of narrow cord (hat)
- One small wooden bead for cord
- Brown and pink acrylic paints
- Black fine-point permanent marker

*(continued)*

### Instructions

Finished dolls are 14 inches tall.

*Note:* Machine zigzag-stitch clothing pieces to body pieces *before* sewing dolls together.

Enlarge the pattern pieces, *below,* onto tissue paper. Add ¼ inch for seam allowances. *Note:* The pattern pieces are shown for assembled doll. Cut a leotard pattern *separate* from ballerina body; cut yoke, shirt, and pants patterns *separate* from cowboy body. For hat back, cut on solid lines. For hat front, cut along dashed line. Add ¼-inch seams.

**Body:** Cut front body shapes *only* from muslin.

**Face:** Transfer facial features and hair (for cowboy *only*) to heads using dressmaker's carbon paper. Draw over all of the lines, *except for the cheeks,* with a black or brown permanent fine-tip marking pen.

When marking pen lines are dry, paint the middle section of the eyes blue (or brown), and the cheeks pink, being careful to paint around the smile line. (Thin the acrylic paints with water so the paint spreads onto the fabric easily. Practice painting on scrap fabric first. See page 77 for painting tips.) Allow paint to dry.

Cut all remaining body pieces from muslin, *except* cut the cowboy's arms from shirt fabric and the cowboy's legs from blue pants fabric.

Cut all of the remaining clothing pieces from appropriate fabrics (see materials list, *page 21*). Set clothing pieces aside.

**For the ballerina:** Baste the leotard and slipper pieces in place; zigzag-stitch pieces to body front and back pattern pieces with blue thread.

**For the cowboy:** Pin clothes to the body front in the following order: shirt, yoke (tuck the fringe beneath yoke), grosgrain ribbon placket, and pants.

Baste all pieces in place; zigzag-stitch to doll body.

Add details and topstitching to the jeans using contrasting thread.

Repeat this procedure for back pattern pieces. Set both sections aside.

## Appliquéd
## Pals
*(continued)*

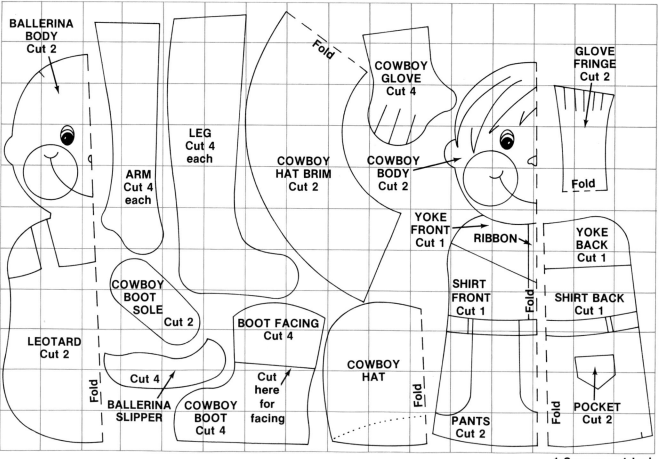

BALLERINA BODY Cut 2

LEG Cut 4 each

ARM Cut 4 each

COWBOY HAT BRIM Cut 2

COWBOY GLOVE Cut 4

COWBOY BODY Cut 2

GLOVE FRINGE Cut 2

Fold

LEOTARD Cut 2

COWBOY BOOT SOLE Cut 2

Fold

BALLERINA SLIPPER

COWBOY BOOT Cut 4

Cut 4

BOOT FACING Cut 4

Cut here for facing

COWBOY HAT

Fold

YOKE FRONT Cut 1

RIBBON

YOKE BACK Cut 1

SHIRT FRONT Cut 1

Fold

SHIRT BACK Cut 1

PANTS Cut 2

Fold

POCKET Cut 2

**1 Square = 1 Inch**

**To assemble both dolls:** Place two arm sections together, with right sides facing; stitch together, leaving the "shoulder" end open for turning.

Trim seams, clip curves, and turn to the right side. Repeat for other arms.

Stuff arms lightly. Do not slip-stitch opening closed.

Repeat arm procedure for legs, *except* turn under ¼ inch on the top of the legs at the opening and slip-stitch opening closed.

Place front and back body sections together, with right sides facing.

Make a small tuck at the open end of each arm. Place the arms inside the doll just below the shoulder curve so that the raw edges of the arms are even with the raw edges of the body pieces.

Pin and stitch the body pieces together, leaving the bottom edge open for stuffing. Trim seams, clip curves, and turn to the right side. Stuff firmly with polyester fiberfill.

Slip-stitch the opening closed, and tack legs to the body.

**To finish the dolls: Ballerina:** String tiny pearls on a 6-inch length of doubled thread. Place the pearls around neckline and tack them to the neck in back. Slip-stitch 10 inches of sequin trim to leotard top.

Cut tulle into two 7x36-inch pieces. Place one atop the other and fold in half lengthwise.

Hand- or machine-baste along the folded edge; gather tulle to fit around the waistline and slip-stitch in place.

*For hair,* cut forty 30-inch lengths of brown yarn. Cut a strip of muslin to measure 1½x3 inches.

Center yarn strands along 3-inch strip; machine-stitch down center of yarn strands, making sure the yarn covers muslin strip completely. (The stitching becomes the center part.)

Tack the wig to the doll's head. Then gather yarn into two ponytails just below the ears. Separate the ponytails into three equal parts and braid. Trim yarn ends evenly. Secure the braids.

Twist each braid into a bun on either side of the ballerina's head and stitch in place. Cut narrow blue ribbon into 12-inch lengths and tie into bows; tack in place.

**Cowboy:** Sew four small buttons to the shirt front along grosgrain ribbon placket.

To add dimples to the elbows and knees, hand-sew a tuck through all thicknesses several times, pulling the thread tightly; knot. Or, machine-stitch across knee and elbow joints.

*Hat:* With right sides facing, sew the front to the back along the curved edge; turn to right side, trim seams and clip curves.

With right sides facing, sew the straight edges of each brim piece together, forming two closed circles.

With right sides facing, stitch the circles together along one circular edge. Turn to right side. Topstitch the outer brim ¼ inch from the edge.

Sew brim to hat, placing brim seam at the center back of hat.

Cut a 12-inch length of brown cord for chin strap; tack one end underneath hat at seam line. Tack other end of cord to opposite side of hat. Pinch cord together at center. Slip a small wooden bead over the double thickness of cord; secure.

Wrap brown cord around base of crown twice; secure. Tack the hat to head, if desired.

*Boots:* With right sides together, sew side edges of boots. Trim seams and clip curves.

Sew the soles to bottom of boots. Turn to the right side.

Sew side seams of facings. With right sides together, slip facing over boot. Sew around the top edges and turn the facing to the inside of the boot. Slip boots onto feet.

*Gloves:* With right sides facing, sew gloves together, leaving the top open. Trim seams and clip curves; turn gloves to the right side.

Wrap fringe around the outside of the top of the glove and stitch together close to one side of the glove. Pull gloves onto doll's hands and topstitch finger lines through all thicknesses.

*Scarf:* Cut a large triangle from red and white gingham and hem all sides. Tie the scarf around the doll's neck, pulling the knot to one side.

Loop fine white cording into a lasso. Then stitch the lasso to the palm of the doll's glove.

# C·O·U·N·T·R·Y  R·A·G  D·O·L·L

**I**f the art of making dolls is a new experience for you, start with a doll that's easy-to-make and is sure to be a hit—this country-fresh lass. Her uncomplicated clothes and body are simple to stitch, and the homespun look requires a minimum of detail. Country Rag Doll is a precious little muffin, and certain to please a favorite daughter, niece, or grandchild.

## Materials

- ⅓ yard of muslin
- ⅔ yard of gray pin-dot fabric
- Scraps of brown broadcloth and rose-and-gray floral print fabric
- 1 small button
- ½ ounce of beige yarn
- Pink and dark brown embroidery floss
- Polyester fiberfill
- Dressmaker's carbon paper
- Tissue paper

## Instructions

Finished size is 13 inches tall.

Enlarge patterns, *right,* onto tissue paper and cut out.

On tissue paper, draw additional patterns measuring 6½x15½ inches (apron skirt), 2¼x3 inches (bib), 1⅛x15½ inches (sash and straps), 1⅛x6½ inches (collar), ¾x4⅝ inches (hair guide), 1¼ inches square (pocket), and 6 inches square (scarf). All the patterns include ¼-inch seam allowances.

Cut out arms and apron from muslin, the dress and one collar from gray pin-dot, legs from brown broadcloth, and headscarf and pocket from floral print. *Note:* Scarf and pocket are used with raw edges exposed.

Transfer torso pattern and facial features onto muslin, using dressmaker's carbon. Embroider features with two strands of floss, using brown for eyes and brows, and pink for nose, mouth, and chin. Color cheeks with rouge. Cut out torso pieces.

**To assemble body:** Place corresponding pieces of torso, each arm, and each leg together, right sides facing. Stitch around, leaving open tops of arms and legs, bottom of torso, and seam at shoulder of torso. Clip the curves, turn, and press.

Stuff arms with fiberfill. With thumbs pointing inward, pinch seam at inside elbow to slightly crook arm; tack in place. Insert arms; stitch in place.

Stuff body and legs. Insert legs into torso and stitch along bottom edge.

**Hair:** Cut guide from muslin. Wind yarn around 12-inch piece of cardboard until hank is 3 inches thick. Cut yarn at each end. Center yarn crosswise along muslin strip and distribute strands evenly along its length. Stitch along center of strip; fold ends under. Stitch to head. Bring several strands of hair to front of head (bangs); trim.

**Clothing: Dress:** Hem short sides and one long collar side. With wrong side of dress and right side of collar together, sew collar to dress. Clip curves, turn collar through the neck opening, and press.

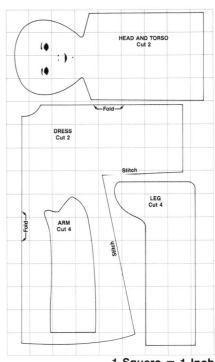

HEAD AND TORSO Cut 2

Fold

DRESS Cut 2

Stitch

LEG Cut 4

Fold

ARM Cut 4

Stitch

**1 Square = 1 Inch**

With right sides together, sew arm and side seams of dress. Clip corners, turn, and press. Hem bottom edge and sleeves.

**For apron:** Hem bottom and sides of apron skirt. Gather top edge, and pin to sash along center 8 inches. (*Note:* Remainder of sash is used for straps.) Stitch apron skirt to sash. Press seam up, then press remaining raw edge under ¼ inch. Fold sash in half lengthwise, matching the folded edges; topstitch along folds to conceal all raw edges.

Hem top and sides of bib; stitch to apron skirt. Stitch pocket in place.

Put dress on doll, and secure at neckline by tying yarn directly over collar seam with collar up. Knot; fold collar down over strip, adjusting gathers. Tack points of collar in place.

Put apron over dress; secure at back sash with small button tacked through overlapped sash. Crisscross straps over shoulders and tack to bib.

**For scarf:** Fold headscarf in half diagonally and place over head; tie in back and tack in place. Trim hair.

# M·O·P  T·O·P

**G**angly arms and legs and a heartfelt smile make this mischievous moppet the immediate friend of toddlers and teens alike. The body construction is simple—just use a knitting needle to ease stuffing into the fingers and toes. Then add a mop of red yarn hair to bring this personable pal to life right before your eyes.

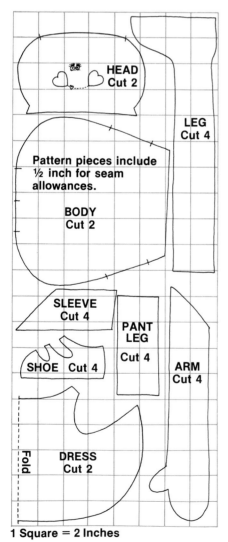

Pattern pieces include ½ inch for seam allowances.

**HEAD** Cut 2

**LEG** Cut 4

**BODY** Cut 2

**SLEEVE** Cut 4

**PANT LEG** Cut 4

**SHOE** Cut 4

**ARM** Cut 4

**DRESS** Cut 2

Fold

1 Square = 2 Inches

## Materials

- ⅓ yard of white fabric (head, arms, and legs)
- ½ yard of peach print fabric (body, sleeves, and pant legs)
- ⅓ yard of blue floral print fabric (dress)
- 1½ yards of 1-inch-wide peach eyelet
- 1¼ yards of 1-inch-wide white eyelet
- 1⅔ yards of ⅛-inch-wide peach satin ribbon
- Scrap of black felt (shoes)
- 1 pound of polyester fiberfill
- 3 skeins of red-orange craft yarn (hair)
- Red and black embroidery floss
- Scrap of red felt (heart cheeks)
- Thread to match
- Dressmaker's carbon paper
- Brown paper
- Embroidery hoop and needle

## Instructions

Finished doll is 33 inches high.

Enlarge pattern pieces, *left,* onto brown paper; cut out. Pattern pieces include ½-inch seam allowances.

**Body: Arms:** Cut the arms from white fabric. Stitch arms together (in pairs), with right sides facing. Clip curves, turn to the right side, and press. Stuff arms firmly with polyester fiberfill.

**Legs:** Cut the legs from white fabric; cut shoe pieces from black felt. Baste one shoe piece to each leg.

With right sides facing, stitch legs together (in pairs), leaving an opening at the top for turning. Clip the seams, turn, and press. Stuff legs firmly.

**Face:** Trace the head pattern onto white fabric; transfer facial features to head pattern using dressmaker's carbon paper. Do not cut out until embroidery is completed.

Place fabric in embroidery hoop. Use two strands of floss for embroidery work. With red floss, work the grin in running stitches and the heart-shaped mouth in satin stitches. With black floss, outline the eyes in backstitches; make a French knot in each eye center. Use straight stitches for the eyelashes. Cut out two heart shapes from red felt for cheeks; machine-appliqué in place. Cut out the head sections.

**Body and head:** Cut body pieces from peach print fabric. Stitch one head section to each body piece; sew head/body pieces together, leaving openings for inserting arms and legs and an opening at the top of the head for stuffing (see markings on pattern). Turn the body section right side out.

**Clothing: Sleeves and pant legs:** Cut patterns from peach print fabric. Hem bottom edge of each pant leg and sleeve.

With right sides facing, stitch the sleeves together (in pairs) along the long sides. Trim the seams, turn to the right side, and press. Repeat procedure for pant legs. Add lace to the lower edge of sleeves and pant legs.

Pin the sleeves and pant legs over arms and legs. Insert limbs into body; stitch in place. Stuff body firmly. Slip-stitch top of head closed. Slip-stitch white eyelet trim around neckline.

**Dress:** Cut two dresses from blue print fabric. Stitch together with right sides facing, leaving an opening for turning. Turn, press, and slip-stitch the opening closed. Add 1-inch-wide peach eyelet trim to the top and bottom edges of the dress. Add ⅛-inch-wide peach ribbon to the back of the dress for neck and waistline ties. Place dress on doll and tie ribbons.

Sew a small pocket to the dress front if desired.

**Hair:** Separate yarn into long bundles of seven strands each. In each bundle, tie overhand knots every 7 inches. Working back and forth across the head from the forehead to the nape of the neck, tack knots close together so yarn forms loops. Leave yarn loops between knots free to stand up in curls.

# C·I·R·C·U·S  C·L·O·W·N

**J**ust imagine the squeals of joy you'll hear from the lucky recipient of this lovable clown! Our colorful, shaggy-haired pal, with his fantastic clothes and zany red and green fingernails, is as jolly as his real-life circus counterpart. He's a wonderful playmate, even for kids who don't like dolls. (Don't be surprised if the "grown up" kids want to play with him, too!)

Embroider the clown's face in colors as vivid as greasepaint itself. (We've included a full-size pattern to help you make his merry face just right.) Then, dig into your ragbag for the brightest scraps you can find to make his imaginative costume.

## Materials
- 1 yard of 44-inch-wide white cotton/polyester broadcloth
- ¾ yard of fabric (pants)
- Small pieces of various other fabrics (blouse, hat, and legs)
- Scraps of red velvet (buttons)
- Scrap of red satin (nose)
- 1½ skeins of rug yarn (hair)
- Scraps of interfacing
- Embroidery floss (facial details and fingernails)
- 2 pounds of polyester fiberfill
- ¼-inch-wide elastic; snaps
- Blue and white seed beads
- Dressmaker's carbon paper
- Embroidery hoop and needle

## Instructions
Finished size is 32 inches high.

Enlarge pattern pieces, *page 31,* onto tissue paper; cut out. Cut the following rectangles from tissue paper: 2½x12 inches (sleeve ruffle), 3½x18 inches (collar), 2½x36 inches (suit ruffle). *Note:* All pattern pieces include ¼-inch seam allowances.

Transfer arms, body front, back, and head pieces onto white broadcloth with dressmaker's carbon paper. *Do not cut out.*

Cut leg pieces from striped fabric. Cut pants pieces from solid fabric.

Cut blouse front from a print fabric; cut two blouse backs from same pattern piece. Cut suit ruffle and collar facings from same fabric. Cut collar, sleeve top, and two sleeve ruffles from coordinating print fabric. Cut sleeve bottom and hat piece on fold from a coordinating solid fabric.

Cut nose circle from red satin and buttons from red velvet. Cut shoe and sole pieces from dark velveteen. Cut two head patterns from interfacing.

**Body: Face and head:** Trace full-size face pattern, *page 30,* onto tissue paper. Draw a line down center of facial features. Set aside.

Stitch a muslin prototype of the two face patterns. Transfer facial features to prototype using dressmaker's carbon. Cut face apart. Draw over features with dark fabric pen.

Lay white fabric over muslin patterns; trace patterns onto white fabric using water-erasable marking pen. Do not cut out head patterns yet.

Baste interfacing to head pieces.

Use two strands of floss for all embroidery. Work satin stitches for all features, unless noted, *below.*

Make the mouth red, cheeks pink, eyebrows red, eyelids variegated orange, eyelash accent purple, and the "dimples" yellow. Outline eyes with flesh-colored split stitches. Embroider pupil with black satin stitches; shade iris with two colors of blue. Add a blue and white seed bead to each pupil for accents. (See page 79 for embroidery stitch diagrams.)

Cut out all head pattern pieces. Place right sides of the embroidered pieces together, and stitch the center-marked sides together.

Gather nose circle with running stitches; stuff with fiberfill and pull thread tight. Sew nose to head.

With right sides together, stitch the remaining two head pieces to head front along side edges. Set aside.

**Arms:** Embroider the fingernails on arms, making one set red and one set green. Cut out arms. With right sides facing, stitch arms together; leave open at top for turning. Clip seams. Turn to right side; stuff arm.

*(continued)*

**Full-size features**

## Circus Clown
*(continued)*

**Legs:** Stitch together the shoe pieces along the back edge. Open and pin the bottom shoe edge to the sole; stitch in place.

Stitch the ankle edge of the leg to the shoe top. Stitch the top of the shoe together; stitch leg seam. Turn.

Stuff the shoe and lower leg; machine-stitch across the "knee," creating a joint. Stuff the upper leg.

**To assemble the body:** Stitch the darts in the back pieces.

Assemble body front by stitching the two center sides together. With right sides together, pin a body piece to the front assembly along the side edge. Stitch to notch, insert the arm in

the seam, and finish the seam. Repeat for other side and arm.

Beginning at lower edge, stitch back seam, leaving a 2½-inch opening at top. Insert legs along bottom edge of body, positioning each leg in 2 inches from side seam. Stitch lower edge of body, securing legs in place.

Pin head inside assembled body. With right sides facing, stitch head to body along neck edge. This leaves half of the body back and back of head open for turning.

Turn to right side and slip-stitch seam closed. Stuff head firmly. Stuff body; slip-stitch neck seam closed.

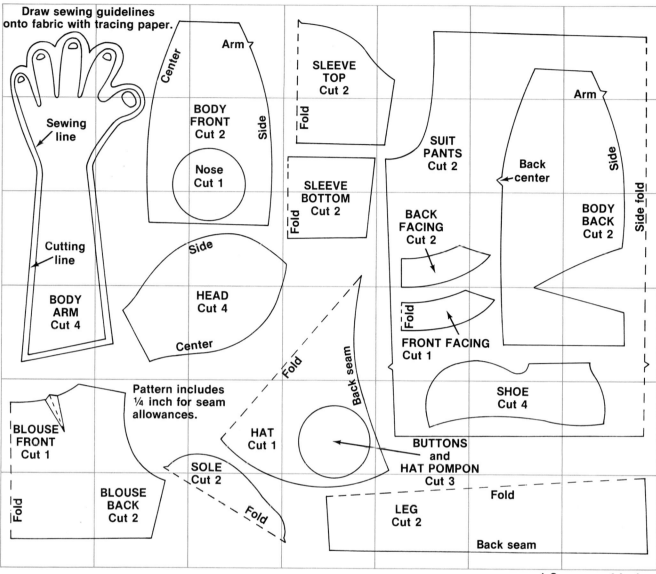

Draw sewing guidelines onto fabric with tracing paper.

Sewing line

Cutting line

**BODY ARM Cut 4**

**BODY FRONT Cut 2**

Center

Arm

Side

**Nose Cut 1**

Side

**HEAD Cut 4**

Center

Arm

**SLEEVE TOP Cut 2**

Fold

**SLEEVE BOTTOM Cut 2**

Fold

**SUIT PANTS Cut 2**

**BACK FACING Cut 2**

Fold

**FRONT FACING Cut 1**

Back center

Side

Side fold

**BODY BACK Cut 2**

**SHOE Cut 4**

Pattern includes ¼ inch for seam allowances.

**BLOUSE FRONT Cut 1**

Fold

**BLOUSE BACK Cut 2**

**SOLE Cut 2**

Fold

**HAT Cut 1**

Fold

Back seam

**BUTTONS and HAT POMPON Cut 3**

Fold

**LEG Cut 2**

Back seam

**1 Square = 4 Inches**

**Clothing: Hat:** Stitch hat piece along back curved seam. Turn under raw edges along bottom edge and stitch in place.

Cut hat pompon circle from a fabric scrap; gather around edges with running stitches. Stuff with fiberfill and pull up gathering thread. Tack to the point of the hat. Set hat aside.

**Blouse:** With the right sides facing, place blouse front and backs together; stitch along shoulder seams.

Finish one long edge of sleeve ruffle. Gather remaining long edge; fit along bottom of sleeve top. Set aside.

Hem the lower (shorter) edge of the sleeve bottom piece.

Place ruffle that was fitted to sleeve atop the lower sleeve, raw edges

even. Baste pieces together. With right sides facing, place basted ruffle and lower sleeve piece atop sleeve top. Stitch all three pieces together.

Next, sew sleeves to blouse front and back, right sides facing. Then fold together blouse front and back, right sides facing, and stitch side and underarm seams. Clip seam at armpit. Affix interfacing to calico front and back facing pieces. Sew facings together at shoulders.

Make suit buttons as directed for hat pompons; stitch to blouse front.

Stitch lower half of back shirt seam together. Turn shirt; press. Fold under remaining raw edges at back neck opening; topstitch. Tack snap fasteners along back opening.

**Pants:** Place the two pants pieces right sides together; sew one curved crotch seam. (This will be the center front seam.) Gather across the top edges. Finish cuff edges. Sew elastic between notches inside pant legs.

Finish one long edge of suit ruffle. Sew ruffle to bottom edge of blouse.

Attach the pants to the blouse, matching the front seam of the crotch to the center of the shirt. Stitch the center back pants seam. Sew up center leg seam; turn. Dress doll.

**Hair:** Using rug yarn, stitch turkey knots on top of the head; make the loops on the knots about 8 inches long. (Wrap yarn loops around a 4-inch-wide cardboard strip.) Clip the loops; trim ends. Tack hat to head.

# VERY SMALL FOLK

Welcome to our small world, where you can create diminutive playthings and gifts from a host of materials. You'll meet the miniature family shown here, plus dolls fashioned from clay, nuts, or your fanciest embroidery—even a pair of Wild West characters made out of string. Instructions begin on page 34.

# D·O·L·L·H·O·U·S·E   F·A·M·I·L·Y

**O**ur old-fashioned family (shown actual size on pages 32 and 33) is detailed enough to please a devoted collector. And with bendable pipe cleaners in the arms and legs, the dolls are ideal for playtime as well.

## Materials
### Bodies
(Yardage is for 45-inch-wide fabric.)
- ⅛ yard of unbleached muslin
- Small amount of polyester fiberfill
- Twenty-one 12-inch-long chenille stems (body frames)—available at craft supply stores
- ⅛ yard of polyester fleece (body padding)
- 2¼ yards of cotton-filled ecru cord (body covering)—available at larger fabric stores
- 1 package of single-fold ecru bias tape

### Girl
- 2¾x6½ inches of white fabric (pantaloons)
- 6½ inches of ¼-inch-wide white lace
- 2¾x18½ inches of red pin-dot fabric (dress)
- 2¾x10½ inches of striped white fabric (pinafore)
- 25½ inches of ¼-inch-wide red and white embroidered trim
- 2¼x2½ inches of white felt (hat)
- 28 inches of ⅛-inch-wide red satin ribbon
- Artificial flowers; green floral tape
- Black felt (shoes)
- 1 skein of brown embroidery floss (hair)
- Brown, red sewing thread (face)
- Powdered rouge

### Grandmother
- 3½x6½ inches of white cotton fabric (pantaloons)
- 4x21 inches of blue dotted fabric (dress)
- 11x15 inches of blue striped fabric (apron)
- 8½ inches of ⅛-inch-wide blue satin ribbon
- 27½ inches of ¼-inch-wide white lace
- Red and green embroidery floss
- Black felt (shoes)
- 2 skeins of gray floss (hair)
- Blue, rose sewing thread (face)
- Powdered rouge

### Mother
- 3½x6½ inches of white cotton fabric (pantaloons)
- 4x21 inches of green calico (dress)
- 1 yard of ¼-inch-wide green velvet ribbon
- 2-inch-square of white fabric (yoke)
- 3 tiny seed pearls
- 31 inches of ¼-inch-wide white lace
- Black felt (shoes)
- 2 skeins of rust floss (hair)
- Blue and rust thread (face)
- Powdered rouge

### Boy
- 4½x5¼ inches of gingham (shirt)
- 2¾x11 inches of blue denim (cap and overalls)
- 4½-inch-square of red calico (bandanna)
- Black felt (shoes)
- 2 skeins of rust floss (hair)
- Blue, rust sewing thread (face)
- Powdered rouge

### Father
- 4½x6½ inches of pinstripe (shirt)
- 3½ inches of ¼-inch-wide brown ribbon (tie)
- 4½x5 inches of brown lightweight wool (trousers)
- 3x7 inches *each* of checked wool (vest) and brown cotton (lining)
- 3 black seed beads (buttons)
- Black felt (shoes)
- 1 skein of brown floss (hair)
- Brown, rust sewing thread (face)
- Powdered rouge

## Instructions
### Body construction
*Note:* Refer to page 42 for tips on making miniature dolls.

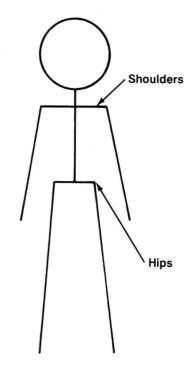

Shoulders

Hips

| | Father | Grandmother and mother | Boy and girl |
|---|---|---|---|
| **Height** | 6" | 5" | 4" |
| **Body*** | 1¾" | 1⅝" | 1½" |
| **Arms**** | 6¾" | 5¾" | 4¾" |
| **Legs**** | 8½" | 6¾" | 6" |
| **Hip** | 1" | ⅞" | ⅞" |
| **Shoulders** | 1⅛" | 1" | 1" |

*From base of neck to crotch. **From tip to tip before ends are bent back to form hands and feet.

34

Body construction is identical for all dolls. See diagram, *opposite.*

Refer to the chart, *opposite below,* for doll measurements before cutting the body pieces and to shape each doll body.

To pad bodies, cut fleece into ⅜-inch-wide strips. Use strips to wrap each stem tightly and smoothly, overlapping fleece every ⅛ inch.

Remove filler from cord before inserting stems.

Enlarge patterns onto tissue paper; cut out.

**Heads:** Trace head patterns onto muslin. Embroider faces before cutting head patterns from fabric (see specific doll instructions for embroidery how-to). Cut pieces from muslin.

Stitch pieces together with right sides facing, unless indicated, *below.*

Stitch head pieces together along curved edge, using small stitches. Trim seam allowance, clip curves, and turn to right side.

Use a double strand of thread to sew a row of gathering stitches ¼ inch from the top; leave needle attached. *Note:* For girl and boy, sew gathering stitches ⅜ inch from top.

Stuff head firmly, keeping bottom round and smooth. Pull gathering stitches tight, closing the opening; secure thread. Trim excess fabric.

**Necks and torsos:** Bend one 7-inch stem in half and twist together. Wrap stems with fleece, leaving ⅜ inch of the bent end unwrapped. Secure end of fleece.

Slip stem into a piece of cord. Stitch bent end of stem to back of head, ⅜ inch from gathered top.

**Arms and hands:** Cut two stems for each pair and twist together (see chart for measurements). Wrap with fleece, ending ¾ inch from each end. Secure fleece.

**Hands:** Bend each end back ⅜ inch. Slip stem into a piece of cord, allowing an extra ¼ inch of cord at each end. Pin ¼ inch of cord to the inside. Slip-stitch together, giving the hands a rounded shape.

Align center of arm/hand piece atop shoulder position on head and body piece. Tightly wrap each arm once around the body. Pinch joining with pliers to secure. Bend shoulders.

**Legs and feet:** Cut two stems for each pair; twist together. Wrap with fleece, ending 1 inch from each end; secure. For feet, bend each end back ½ inch. Slip stem into piece of cord, leaving feet uncovered.

Align center of leg piece across lower body part. Check body length and tightly wrap body piece once between legs. Continue to wrap end of body piece around upper part of body. Bend at hip and bend feet flat.

**Torsos:** To pad torso, wrap with fleece, beginning at top. Wrap over shoulders several times.

Shape the top of the body broader and keep the waist narrow. *Note:* Make the body fuller at the bustline for the grandmother and mother.

Wrap one short piece of bias tape over each shoulder, crisscrossing over front and back; secure ends.

Wrap bias tape between legs from waist front to waist back; secure.

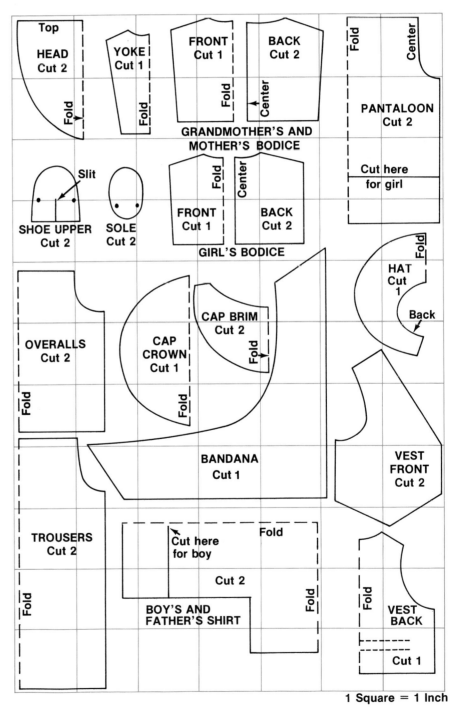

1 Square = 1 Inch

35

# Dollhouse Family

*(continued)*

Completely wrap body with bias tape from chest to top of legs, overlapping tape every ¼ inch; turn end of bias tape under at back and secure.

All pattern pieces include ¼ inch for seam allowances. Use matching thread throughout, unless otherwise indicated. Hand sewing may simplify some parts of the clothing constructions, due to the small size of pattern pieces. All embroidery floss for the hair is used in its original circular shape. *Do not unwind.*

**Grandmother: Face:** Embroider features as desired, using a single strand of sewing thread and following colors suggested in materials list.

Satin-stitch eyes, shaping them in a round, oval, or crescent shape. With straight stitches, work nostrils, dimples, eyelashes at outer edges of eyes, and lips into smiles. Color the cheeks with powdered rouge.

**Hair:** For center part, stitch across the center of one skein of floss, making the stitching ⅞ inch long. Stitch skein of floss to head along part.

Wrap the two ends of the skein to back of neck and head, tacking hair at sides of face to sculpt curved bangs; stitch floss to head at neck. Sew looped ends to back and top of head, keeping floss flat and smooth and completely covering the head.

For the bun, cut one skein into two equal pieces. Using only one piece, twist the strands tightly. Overlap the ends, forming a loop; neatly secure ends together. Twist loop in center, forming two smaller loops. Fold one loop atop the other and pin to top of head; stitch in place.

Spray hair with spray starch. Wrap head with strip of thin plastic wrap to hold until starch is dry. Repeat spray-and-wrap method until floss is set.

**Pantaloons:** Cut pantaloon pieces from white fabric. Press leg hems under ¼ inch, slip lace under hem, and stitch together.

Stitch center fronts together, and stitch center backs together. Stitch front to back. Clip curves; press.

Stitch inner legs together. Clip at each side of center; press and turn.

Press under ¼ inch of top edge. Sew a row of gathering stitches along top edge. Place pantaloons on doll; pull gathers to fit and secure. Tack pantaloons to doll at center back.

**Shoes:** From black felt, cut soles, upper pieces, and two ½x1½-inch leg pieces. Pin one upper piece to each sole, matching dots. Whipstitch together around front of shoe from dot to dot. Place shoe on doll. Finish whipstitching upper piece to sole; stitch backs together. Stitch the leg pieces around top of shoe, matching backs. Tack leg piece to shoe.

**Dress:** Cut front and back bodice pieces, 4x11½-inch piece (skirt), and two 2¼x2¾-inch pieces (sleeves) from blue dotted fabric.

Sew a row of gathering stitches along one long edge of skirt piece. Press under ¼ inch on short sides.

Press under ¼ inch on the center edges of back pieces. Stitch front to backs at shoulders; press seams. Press neck edge to inside. Slip-stitch lace to inside of neck edge, turning ends under at backs.

Press under ¼ inch on one long edge of each sleeve. Slip-stitch row of lace ⅞ inch from pressed edge. Sew gathering stitches along other long edge. Pull gathers, leaving ¼ inch ungathered at each end. Fit and stitch gathered sleeve edge to bodice.

Stitch bodice together at sides and sleeves. Clip at underarm. Stitch skirt to bodice. Stitch center-back seam for 2 inches, starting at skirt bottom.

Press under ¼ inch, then ¾ inch at skirt bottom; hem. Stitch lace to hem. Turn dress to right side.

Place dress on doll. Overlap bodice backs and sew together. Sew gathering stitches at end of each sleeve; pull gathers to fit and secure.

**Apron:** From striped fabric, cut one 3¼x7½-inch-rectangle (for the skirt), one 1x14½-inch-strip (for sash), two 1⅜-inch-squares (for the bib), and two ¾x2¼-inch strips (for straps).

Press under ¼ inch on one long edge of skirt, then press under ¾ inch. Pin ⅜-inch-wide blue ribbon ⅝ inch from pressed edge. Stitch ribbon to skirt, catching hem in stitching.

Press under ¼ inch on short sides to inside twice; stitch together.

Trim skirt with embroidered flowers. With two strands of thread, work three red French knots for flowers, and two green lazy daisy stitches for leaves. Equally space five groups of flowers around skirt.

Gather top of skirt to measure 2½ inches. Fold and press sash into thirds, turning ends of sash to inside. Center sash over gathers; sew from one end of sash to other, stitching close to bottom edge and including skirt in stitching.

Stitch ⅛-inch-wide blue ribbon ⅝ inch from top of one bib piece. Stitch bib front to back around three sides; turn and press. Embroider one flower group above ribbon. Center bib to sash and slip-stitch in place.

Fold and press each strap in thirds. Stitch end of each strap under bib top, matching side edges. Place the apron on the doll. Cross the straps in back and tack straps to the inside of the sash. Tie sash into bow.

**Mother: Face:** Embroider the face as directed for grandmother, using blue and rust sewing threads.

**Hair:** Fashion hair as directed for grandmother, eliminating coiled bun and adding a braided bun instead. To do this, tie one end of one floss skein with thread. Cut other end and divide floss into three equal parts. Braid for 3½ inches; secure end. Overlap ends and sew into circle. Tack in place.

**Pantaloons and shoes:** Cut out and stitch as for grandmother.

**Dress:** From green calico fabric, cut the dress pieces using measurements given for grandmother's dress. Stitch dress in same manner, except for bodice front. Cut yoke from white fabric. Press under ¼ inch on long edges. Center yoke to dress bodice, placing lace under pressed edges. Sew yoke and lace to front. Add seed pearls for buttons. Add lace and velvet trims to skirt and sleeves. Tie velvet ribbon around waist.

**Girl: Face:** Stitch as directed for the grandmother, using brown and red sewing thread.

**Hair:** Fashion part and attach hair to head as directed for grandmother. For pigtails, cut loops at each end of floss. To shape loose bangs, tack several strands of floss to the center front part. Tack several strands of floss to the back of the neck to secure in place. Tie pigtails at base of head. Comb the pigtails to separate and smooth floss; trim ends, and tie pigtails with red bows. Spray the hair as directed for the grandmother doll.

**Pantaloons and shoes:** Cut out and stitch as for grandmother.

**Dress:** From red dot fabric, cut a 2¾x8¾-inch rectangle (skirt), front and back bodice pieces, and two 2¼x2¾ inch pieces (sleeves). Construct dress as for grandmother, with these exceptions: Stitch center back seam for 1½ inches; press under ½ inch for skirt hem.

**Pinafore:** From white striped fabric, cut a 2¾x8¾-inch rectangle (skirt), and 1¼x1½-inch piece (bib).

Press under ½ inch on one long edge of skirt twice. Sew trim ½ inch from pressed edge, catching hem in stitching. Press under ¼ inch on short sides twice; stitch. Sew gathering stitches along top edge. Pull gathers to measure 2¼ inches. For sash, center and pin 11 inches of trim over gathers; stitch in place.

Fold bib piece in half and stitch two long sides together; turn to right side and press. For straps, pin 2½ inches of trim along each outer edge of bib front, beginning trim at raw edges. Stitch together. Join bib to skirt, placing raw edge of bib under sash. Place pinafore on doll. Cross straps in back and tack straps to inside of sash. Tie sash at back into small bow.

**Hat:** Cut hat from white felt. Pin ⅛-inch-wide red ribbon around the inner edge of the hat, allowing an extra ½ inch of ribbon at each end. Stitch ribbon to hat. Tack a narrow ribbon bow and small flowers to hat. Place hat on head, slip-stitching the raw edges of the ribbon under for a snug fit.

Attach spray of flowers, wrapped with floral tape, to palm of hand.

**Father: Face:** Embroider face as directed for grandmother doll, using brown and rust sewing threads.

**Hair:** Cut skein of floss into four equal pieces. For side part, stitch across floss ⅜ inch from center, making stitching line 1⅜ inches long. Stitch in place. Separate floss nearest head into single layer. Sew layer to head along bottom hairline. Lightly comb top layer. Spray with spray starch; shape floss around head; trim to shape. Finish as for grandmother.

**Shoes:** Make as for grandmother.

**Shirt:** Cut one shirt piece, two ¾x1½-inch pieces (cuffs), and one 1x2-inch piece (collar).

Press under ¼ inch of the center backs, tapering to nothing at center front. Stitch shirt together at sides and sleeves. Clip at underarm; press the seams and turn. Place shirt on doll, overlap backs, and secure.

Sew gathering stitches at sleeve ends. Gather to fit; secure to arm. Fold and press cuffs over sleeve gathers. Slip-stitch cuff to sleeve.

Press under ¼ inch on each long edge of collar. Stitch each short end together. Turn to right side, press, slip-stitch open edge closed. Pin and tack tops of collar to shirt; tack to center front. Tie narrow brown ribbon into loose knot in center; tack to shirt.

**Trousers:** Cut trousers from fabric. Turn under ¼ inch on pant legs; hem. Stitch center fronts together. Stitch ¼ inch of the center backs together, starting at bottom. Clip curves; press.

Stitch inner legs together, matching center seams. Clip at each side of center. Press seams and turn.

Press under ¼ inch of top edge. Put trousers on doll. Slip-stitch center back seam; tack trousers to doll.

**Vest:** Cut vest pieces from fabric.

Stitch back to back lining, leaving a 1-inch opening at the bottom. Trim seams, clip curves, and turn to right side. Press; stitch opening closed.

Stitch fronts to linings, making one left front and one right front; leave V-neck open for turning. Trim seams, clip curves, and turn to right side. Press and slip-stitch openings closed.

Slip-stitch shoulders and sides together. Sew beads to left front. Stitch two rows of gathering stitches on the back. Place vest on doll; pull gathers to fit and secure. Secure in front.

**Boy: Face:** Embroider face as for grandmother, using blue and rust threads.

**Hair:** Cut each skein into four equal pieces. Stack three pieces together for each section (only two sections are used). Stitch across one section 1¼ inches from one end, making stitching 1¼ inches long. Slip-stitch the stitching to head from ear to ear. Separate floss nearest head into a single layer; sew to head along bottom hairline. With second section, stitch across center of floss, making stitching ⅝ inch long. Pin to head, placing stitching as for center part; sew in place. Comb floss; trim bangs, sides, and bottom, and layer hair. Spray with starch as for grandmother.

**Shoes:** Cut out and stitch as directed for grandmother.

**Overalls:** Cut the overalls, a 1-inch-square (bib), and two ¾x2½-inch pieces (straps) from blue denim.

Press under ¼ inch to hem pant legs. Topstitch with orange thread.

Stitch center front seams together. Starting at the bottom, stitch center back seams together for ¼ inch. Clip curves and press seams. Press under ¼ inch of top edge.

Stitch inner legs together. Clip at each side of center; press and turn.

Press under ¼ inch on three sides of bib. Topstitch folded edges with orange thread. Pin bib to overalls; topstitch the folded edge of overalls, catching bib in stitching. Work orange French knots for buttons.

Fold and press straps into thirds; topstitch the long edges with orange thread. Sew straps under bib top.

Place overalls on doll. Cross straps in back and tack in place. Slip-stitch center back seam.

**Shirt:** Cut shirt and two ¾x1½-inch bias cuffs from gingham.

Stitch shirt as directed for father.

**Bandanna:** Cut out bandanna; hem and tie to doll.

**Cap:** Cut pieces from denim. Sew gathering stitches around outer edge of crown; pull gathers. Stitch brims together along outer edge. Clip the curves, turn, and press. Topstitch brim with orange thread. Stitch brim to crown. Pin gathered edge under and slip-stitch cap to head.

37

# S·C·U·L·P·T·U·R·E·D  C·H·E·R·U·B·S

**T**hese baby dolls are so much fun to make that you may end up with a houseful! The heads are shaped from special clay, then painted and attached to fabric bodies. Tie the dressed and diapered babies to shower gifts to delight a mother-to-be.

## Materials
- ¼ yard of print fabric
- ¼ yard of flesh-colored fabric
- Scrap of white flannel (diaper)
- ⅔ yard of ⅛-inch-wide ribbon
- Lace; snap
- Oven-firing clay (head)
- Polyester fiberfill
- Fine-point permanent marker, acrylic paints (facial features)
- Scrap of mohair yarn (hair)
- Clear nail polish
- Scrap of thin round elastic

## Instructions
Dolls measure 6 inches high.

**Head:** Form head with lump of clay the size of a golf ball. Roll it between your hands until smoothly rounded. Attach tiny clay ball for nose, making nostrils with toothpick. Add short clay cylinder for neck. "Drill" two ⅛-inch-diameter holes in neck with a sharp tool so neck can be stitched to body.

Following the manufacturer's directions, harden clay in the oven; cool. Paint face with flesh-colored acrylics.

Add facial features with permanent marker. Paint the eyes and cheeks. When dry, paint head with clear nail polish; dry.

**Hair:** Pull apart mohair yarn to create fluff. Apply polish to head for placement of hair. Place fluff on head while polish is wet. Set head aside.

**Body:** Enlarge patterns onto tissue paper and cut out. Cut arms, legs, and body from flesh-colored fabric.

*Note:* Stitch pieces together with right sides facing, unless directions indicate otherwise. Allow ⅛ inch for seam allowances.

**Arms:** Stitch the arms together in pairs, leaving an opening for turning. Clip curves, turn, and stuff. Slip-stitch opening closed.

**Legs:** Stitch the legs in the same manner as directed for the arms.

**Body:** Sew two body sections together along center seam for body front. Repeat with remaining sections (body back). Lay body front atop back and stitch together, starting at A and sewing around to neck edge. Leave neck open for turning. Turn, clip curves, and stuff.

**Doll assembly:** Insert head into neck opening; sew in place, using holes in neck for attaching head to body. Add extra stuffing to neck if needed. Cut a ¾-inch-wide strip of body fabric long enough to wrap around neck and to overlap. Fold long edges under and wrap around neck; tack in place.

Slip-stitch legs and arms to body.

**Clothing:** Cut bonnet and dress pieces and one 3x5¾-inch rectangle (skirt) from print fabric.

**Dress:** Stitch front bodice pieces together along the neckline. Turn; sew ribbons to front on pattern lines.

Gather skirt; pull gathers to fit front bodice. Stitch in place; set aside.

Sew back facing to dress back along dashed neckline. Cut the back opening; turn facing inside; press. Stitch front to back at shoulders.

Press under ¼-inch hem on the sleeve. Run elastic inside fold. Stitch elastic in place to one end; sew along edge of elastic, forming a casing. Pull elastic to fit doll arm; secure elastic. Repeat for other sleeve. Gather top edge of each sleeve. Stitch the sleeves in place; sew side seams.

Hem dress. Sew snap to neck opening and dress doll.

**Diaper:** Cut a 4x5-inch piece of white flannel; hem. Pin to doll.

**Bonnet:** Cut bonnet pieces from print fabric. Sew brims together along curved edge. Turn, press, and stitch lace to curved edge.

Press and stitch under ¼ inch on bonnet sides. Sew back facing to bonnet back; turn and press. Sew close to raw edge of facing to form casing. Pull 3 inches of narrow ribbon through casing; tie ends together.

Gather front of bonnet to fit straight edge of brim; sew together. Sew 5-inch lengths of ribbon to each side of bonnet for ties. Tie bonnet on doll. Adjust casing ribbon. Knot ends; trim.

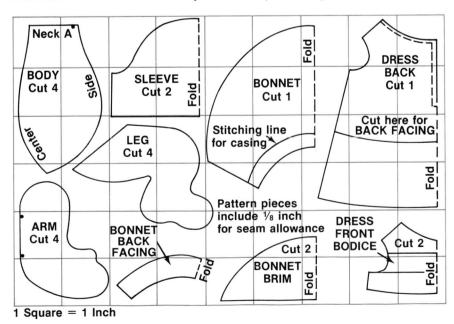

1 Square = 1 Inch

**Full-size features**

# B·A·B·Y  D·O·L·L

## TO SIGN WITH LOVE

**T**his enchanting baby doll comes bearing best wishes for your favorite mother-to-be (and baby, too). It's a gift she'll treasure, because it's personalized by the folks from your office, bridge club, family, or other circle of friends. Just ask everyone to sign their autograph (and add sweet motifs and sayings if they wish) to the muslin pieces that form the lifelike body. Then embroider the signatures and the designs, assemble the doll, and present it with pride to the lucky mom.

### Materials

- 2 yards of 45-inch-wide muslin fabric (body and cap)
- Scrap of white felt
- Small amount of rust mohair yarn (hair)
- Polyester fiberfill
- Washable fabric marking pens
- Scraps of embroidery floss in a variety of colors
- Permanent fine-tip markers in a variety of colors (optional)
- Powdered rouge
- Embroidery hoop
- Embroidery needle
- ⅓ yard of white flannel (diaper)
- Diaper pins
- Ecru eyelet lace
- 28 inches of ⅜-inch-wide yellow satin ribbon

### Instructions

Finished doll, seated, measures 14 inches tall.

*Note:* All of the pattern pieces are assembled with right sides facing, unless stated otherwise. Using small stitches, sew all the body seams twice for added strength.

Preshrink muslin. Enlarge patterns found on page 42. Lay the fabric, right side up, over pattern; trace outlines onto the muslin, using washable fabric marker. All pattern pieces *include* ¼-inch seam allowances; with marker, draw seam lines on muslin. Take care to reverse pattern pieces as necessary. *Do not cut out patterns.*

**Decorating the doll:** The doll pictured here is embroidered with sweet greetings, good wishes, and personal signatures. Be sure to use a washable fabric marker for marking on muslin. *Note:* Be careful to avoid sketching too close to seam allowances or darts, because the designs may be lost when doll is assembled.

Transfer face pattern onto head. Place muslin in embroidery hoop and use three strands of embroidery floss for stitching.

Work satin stitches for the mouth and eyes, straight stitches for eyelashes, and outline stitches for eyelids and nose. Work names and words with backstitches. See page 79 for embroidery stitch diagrams.

When stitching is done, daub fabric with wet cloth to remove blue marks.

*Note:* You may choose to assemble the doll first, and add signatures and designs with colored permanent fine-tip marking pens afterward.

Mark lines on hands and feet and darts on wrong side of muslin. Cut out all pattern pieces.

**To assemble the body:** Stitch darts on front and back pieces; trim darts and press.

Stitch center back seams from the neck top to center of third dart. Clip curves; press. Repeat for center front.

Stitch front to back along shoulders, sides, and bottom, leaving neck open for turning. Clip curves, press, and turn to right side. Pin 1 inch of the neck to the inside; baste ¼ inch from folded edge.

Stuff the body firmly. (Refer to page 23 for tips on stuffing dolls.)

Whipstitch ends of arms to body at shoulder side seams.

For back dimples, use a double strand of thread and a long needle to pull thread from one dimple to the other. Make one small stitch at each dimple and pull the thread tight enough to make an indentation. Repeat back and forth several times.

For the navel, cut a 1¼-inch-diameter circle from muslin. From white felt, cut two ¾-inch-diameter circles. Stack felt circles in center of muslin circle. Fold muslin around felt circles and tack to felt. Tack the navel to the center front.

**Legs:** Stay-stitch along the top of each leg, as marked, to reinforce leg openings. Stitch together center front and center back seams. Clip curves and press seams.

Stitch soles to legs. Slightly round off toe section of the leg to match shape of sole. Clip curves and turn.

Stuff toes moderately. Pin across toe section to separate this area from rest of foot. Stuff foot and leg firmly. Whipstitch top of leg closed.

For knee and heel dimples, use a double strand of thread and pull the thread through limb from one dimple to the other. Make one small stitch at each dimple and pull thread tight enough to make an indentation. Repeat back and forth several times.

**Toes:** Mark toes with pins. Shape toes by sewing a large loop stitch around end of each toe. (Pull needle from bottom of toe to the top and pull thread tightly.) Repeat. Complete the shape of the toes by working back stitches through the top. Sew dimples above each toe.

Whipstitch legs to body, placing them under the front darts.

*(continued)*

To "Mom"
n love from the
gang at work
Bundle
of
Joy
PRIDE & JOY
LITTLE ONE
Laura
good night
Nancy L.
Apple of
Jim

## Baby Doll

*(continued)*

**Arms:** Reinforce arm openings by stay-stitching along top of each arm (see pattern). Transfer finger lines to the wrong side of the left and right hands, with dressmaker's carbon paper. Reinforce the area between the fingers with iron-on interfacing. (This prevents the seam from ripping out after fingers are stuffed.)

Stitch arms together, leaving top open. Restitch inner curves and between each finger. Clip curves and between fingers; trim and turn.

Stuff the fingers and hands moderately. Stuff arms firmly. Slip-stitch the openings closed.

Stitch elbow and hand dimples as for leg dimples. Stitch arms to body.

**Head:** Stitch the darts. Clip open the darts and trim the seams.

Stitch sides of the head to the head front. Clip curves and press.

Sew the head sides to the back, leaving the neck area open. Clip the curves, turn, and stuff head firmly.

Insert 1 inch of the head into the neck opening. Using a double strand of thread, blindstitch the head into place. Add more stuffing if needed.

**Clothing: Diaper:** Cut diaper from white flannel. Transfer the darts to the wrong side of diaper. Stitch darts together. Clip darts, trim, and press. With wrong sides facing, turn up a ⅜-inch hem all around; stitch together ¼ inch from edge.

**Bonnet:** Cut the back piece and a 5¾ x 16-inch rectangle from muslin.

Press under ¼ inch twice on one long edge of rectangle; stitch.

Gather remaining long side, leaving 3 inches ungathered at each end. Stitch back to gathered edge of the rectangular piece. Clip curves.

Press under ½ inch twice on bottom edge. Stitch close to the inner pressed seam to form casing.

Pull ribbon through casing. Slip-stitch eyelet trim to bonnet.

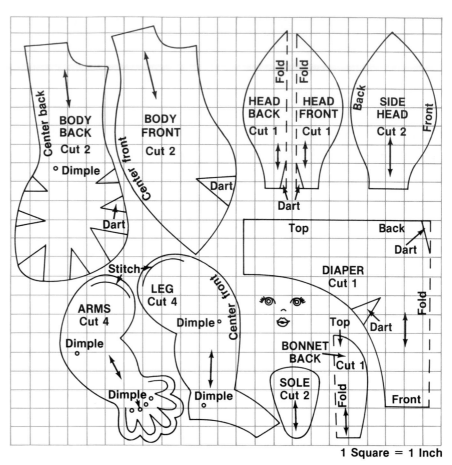

1 Square = 1 Inch

## TIPS FOR MAKING SMALL DOLLS

Small dolls require special crafting skills. Here are tips for making your favorite miniatures.

• Draw around patterns on double thickness of fabric. Sew over drawn lines; cut close to stitching.

• Use 20 stitches per inch for machine-sewing, or sew seams by hand. Trim seams evenly; clip curves at uniform intervals. Iron or finger-press all seams open.

• Use thread or one strand of floss to embroider faces.

• Select prints for clothes and yarn or threads for hair scaled to the size of the doll.

• Spot glue trims and laces in place with fabric glue, then sew.

• For a hat, cut handles off tiny straw basket; invert basket. Trim.

• Make glasses from florist wire and dip into plastic film.

• Make buttons, using a paper punch and colored plastic lids and containers. Heat needle to pierce holes in buttons. Or, use tiny glass beads and seed pearls for buttons.

• For bows, thread ribbon into a needle. Take a stitch in the fabric; pull ribbon through. Remove the needle, tie bow, and secure.

# C·O·U·N·T·R·Y  F·O·L·K

I nspired by primitive dolls of years gone by, these pecan-head figures are as appealing to collectors of Americana as they are to young people. With arms and legs of bendable wire, these dolls are best suited to dollhouse life where the miniatures are just their size.

## Materials

- Smooth, unblemished pecans with medium-to-thick shells
- Medium-weight wire
- Lightweight batting
- Old nylon stockings
- Scraps of fabric, lace, felt and glove leather
- Electric drill; ⅛-inch drill bit
- Adjustable wrench or small vise
- Needle-nose pliers
- Carpet thread
- Clear acrylic spray
- White glue
- Foam plastic block
- Acrylic paints
- Fine brushes
- Toothpicks

## Instructions

**Note: Because of their florist's wire framework, these dolls are not suitable for young children.**

**Doll body: Head:** Grip the nut firmly with an adjustable wrench or in a small vise; drill hole in one end.

Discard nuts that split and crack; drill the nuts until you have enough. Set nuts on toothpicks; insert into a foam block for stability when painting facial features.

(You may wish to experiment with different types of nuts for doll heads.

A walnut will give a wrinkled texture to the face, appropriate for older character dolls. Try using a small round filbert for a baby or tiny child. Brazil nuts also provide interesting texture and shape for faces.)

Using the photograph as a guide, paint simple facial features on nuts. When dry, protect faces with clear spray. Allow to dry thoroughly.

**Body framework:** Cut a wire twice the height of each doll. (Adults are 9 inches tall; boy is 6 inches tall.) Cut a second piece 6 inches long for arms and hands. Bend longer wire in half (folded end will be inserted into head). Fold each wire end (about 1 inch) at right angle, then fold back again ½ inch to make base for foot.

For the arms, wrap a short wire twice around body, about 2 inches below fold of neck. Fold ends under for the hands. Wrap several twists of thread around the arm and body joint.

To fill out the body, cut batting into long 1-inch-wide strips; wrap tightly from shoulder to toes and along arms (do not wrap neck). Secure by wrapping body with thread.

Drip glue into hole in nut. When glue is tacky, insert neck wire into head as far as possible; dry.

Wrap body with 1-inch-wide nylon stocking strips; secure with stitches.

**Clothing:** Dress nut head figures using scraps of fabric, lace, and felt. Use narrow ribbons and tiny pearls or seed beads for trimming.

See tip box, *left,* and the special section on pages 48 and 49 for tips on making and dressing dolls.

# S·T·R·I·N·G  D·O·L·L·S

## ROPED AND TIED

Though the technique may be new to you, there's no trick—rope or otherwise—to making this cable-cord cowpoke and his sassy girlfriend. Simple diagrams show you how to tie up lots of these delightful "pardners" to please all of your favorite Western fans.

## Materials

- Cotton cable cord (available at fabric stores): 1½ yards of size 350 (½-inch diameter) for each doll; 5 yards of size 150 (¼-inch diameter) for each doll
- Assorted colored strings or cording (hair, trims, legs)
- Scraps of white yarn
- Bandanna fabric (cowboy)
- Scraps of white knit fabric (faces)
- 2 yards of polyester/cotton woven cording (basket, hat)
- Black, brown, and pink embroidery floss
- Scraps of polyester fiberfill
- Needle and thread
- White glue
- Food coloring
- Masking tape

## Instructions

**Doll body:** Cut larger cable cord (350) as follows: 12-inch length (arms), 30-inch length (body/legs), and two 5-inch lengths (body). Wrap cut ends with masking tape. Loop 30-inch length and two 5-inch lengths over 12-inch length (see diagram A).

Take smaller cable cord (150) and wrap it around three center cords, beginning at top and continuing under arms for 1½ inches. (The 30-inch length becomes the neck.) Glue end to body (see diagrams B and C). Trim uneven cord *from 5-inch strands only.*

**Legs:** Fold ends of two long leg cords up 2½ inches; secure with tape or tack in place. Wrap leg with colored cord 1¼ inches from loop until raw edge is covered; secure.

**Arms:** Wrap ends of each arm for ½ inch with white yarn. *Girl:* Make loop at arm tops for sleeve; secure.

**Clothing:** Cut ten 12-inch strips of smaller cord. Fold each in half; tack fold to bottom of wrapped waist section. Untwist each strand.

**Skirt:** Tie colored cord around the waist, allowing loose ends to hang down back. Tack bow to neckline.

**Chaps:** Divide the strands in half. With a length of smaller cord, make several figure-eight wraps around the legs directly under the waist, causing legs to bow out; secure. Trim strands.

**Head:** Cut a 3¾-inch-diameter circle from knit fabric. Gather the outside edge. Fill circle with fiberfill and pull gathering thread to close circle; secure thread.

Cut a ¾-inch-diameter circle from knit; gather and stuff for a nose. Tack nose to face. With black embroidery floss, work bullion stitches for eyelids and straight stitches for eye and eyelashes. Cut a small circle of pink felt (mouth); stitch to face using pink straight stitches. Brush cheeks with powdered rouge. *Cowboy:* Omit the eyelashes and the felt mouth. Tack four strands of yarn to the face to create the moustache.

**Hair:** Wrap a long strand of yarn tightly around a size 3 knitting needle without overlapping strands. Fill the entire needle. Place needle on cookie sheet and bake in oven at 375 degrees for 10 minutes. Cool on needle, then slide yarn off. Make enough to cover head; tack yarn to head. Sew head to top of neck section.

**Accessories: Basket:** Using polyester/cotton woven cord, begin the basket by coiling and whipstitching cord into a 1-inch-diameter flat circle. Coil cord up atop the outside edge of the circle until side reaches height of 1½ inches. Stitch cord to inside of basket. Cut cord for handle; knot each end and tack to basket.

**Flowers:** Use leftover cable cord and tie a knot near one end. Fray strands above knot. Dye in food coloring mixed with small amount of water; dry and glue into basket.

**Cowboy hat:** With polyester/cotton woven cord, fold and whipstitch cord into an oval 1 inch long. Build the crown in same manner as the basket, allowing the side of the crown to become wider each time a row of cording is added. When crown measures ¾ inch deep, form brim by winding cord flatly around the brim five times. Tuck cord under brim and secure. Tack hat to head.

**Lariat:** Cut a 13-inch piece of stiff cord. Tie a loop in one end. Attach the lariat to the hand.

### String doll construction

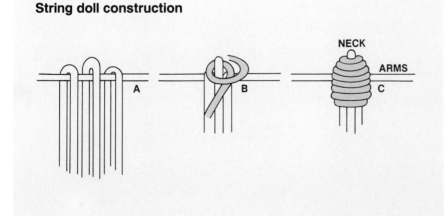

# How to make and dress a perfect doll

Dressing a doll in "designer originals" is easy (and fun, too) when you begin with rectangles, circles, and squares of fabric. That's just what this collection is made from—exclusively! For tips on stitching clothes (and some clever doll-crafting hints), please turn the page.

# How to Make and Dress a Perfect Doll

*(continued)*

Whether you're tackling your first rag doll or designing a sophisticated poppet, these tips will help you turn out a beautiful, professional-looking doll every time. You'll also find useful suggestions for crafting doll clothes similar to those shown on pages 46 and 47, using the simplest of shapes.

## Selecting materials

For the doll body, choose a firm, closely woven fabric. Unbleached muslin is a practical choice, but also consider other fabrics that suggest interesting skin textures and colors. Always select high-quality fabric, because the body fabric will largely determine the doll's quality.

Select body fabric and yarn for the doll's hair first, then use these materials to coordinate fabrics and trims for the clothing. Before beginning construction, lay out all materials to make sure they work well together.

## Cutting and stitching

Lay out the fabric with right sides facing. Unless otherwise indicated, position the longest part of the pattern piece on the lengthwise grain of the fabric.

Instead of cutting out the fabric before stitching, draw around the patterns onto a double thickness of the fabric. Stitch on the drawn line, leaving openings for turning. Then cut out ⅜ inch away from the stitching.

Set your machine for 15 to 20 stitches to the inch, using the 20-stitch setting when sewing tiny areas such as fingers. Double-stitch the seams using matching thread, or thread that is slightly lighter than your fabric.

Press seams flat on both sides, then press open. (Finger-press seams that are too intricate for an iron.) Trim seams evenly; clip the curves at even intervals and close to the stitching.

## Attaching arms and legs

For extra strength, use buttonhole twist or pearl cotton thread to attach limbs to the body.

To add interest, stitch arms to the body with one arm slightly raised or more forward than the other, rather than having the arms perfectly aligned. Use T-pins, which are longer and stronger than regular pins, to hold arms and legs to the body while determining their positions and while hand-stitching the limbs in place.

To make the hands more realistic, pin a small tuck in the palm of the hands; use tiny blind stitches to secure. On a one-piece hand, create fingers by hand-stitching finger lines.

Just for fun, add a dab of powdered rouge to the doll's elbows and knees.

## Facial features

The most important part of a doll is its face, since facial features determine a doll's true personality. Designing the perfect face for your doll takes practice and experimentation, but it will be easier with these guidelines.

**To shape the features:** First study illustrations, photographs, and books about dolls, and dolls you have at home for different types of facial features. Keep a scrapbook of expressions you like, then simplify them to their basic shapes for adaptation to your dolls.

A plastic template of ovals and circles available at art or crafts stores will provide basic shapes that can be used for many facial features. Experiment with different features by cutting small pieces of felt into eye, cheek, and mouth shapes. Cut out and combine the shapes to yield a variety of expressions. (See the section on positioning the features, *below*.)

Pin tracing paper over felt pieces and trace them with a pencil, then transfer the outlines to the face for painting or embroidery. Or, appliqué felt features directly onto the face.

Another way to experiment with facial features is to pencil the face on a piece of muslin, then color the features with crayons. Cut around the face and pin it to the doll's head. Experiment with several combinations of features until the desired effect is achieved. Transfer the pattern to the doll's face.

**To position the features:** Use the following hints as a general guide.

*Eyes:* Position eyes halfway between chin and the top of the head, leaving a space equal to the width of one eye between them.

*Nose:* Place the bottom of the nose halfway between the eyes and chin, or slightly closer to the chin.

*Mouth:* Place it halfway between the nose and the chin.

*Ears:* Position tops of ears even with eyebrows, and the bottoms even with the lower edge of the nose.

*For a child's face,* make the eyes rounder and spaced farther apart. Or, place all of the features lower on a rounder face.

**To apply features:** Use embroidery, paints, appliqué, or a combination of all three techniques.

When painting features on fabric, mix a little white glue with acrylic paint to prevent paint from bleeding into fabric. Using a light touch and small, good quality paintbrushes, practice first on scrap fabric until you achieve the proper paint consistency.

If you embroider the features, use fewer strands of floss or sewing thread to stitch small parts, such as nostrils, eyelashes, and eyebrows.

For appliquéd cheeks, cut circles, hearts, or triangles from red or pink felt or fabric, or embroider cheeks with a circle of running stitches or a smooth circle of satin stitches. Use buttons or beads for a different effect.

To use rouge for cheek color, rub a cotton swab or a small ball of fiberfill into a rouge cake. Gently blow excess rouge from the ball and lightly rub color on the fabric. Repeat if necessary. To keep the color from rubbing off, spray it *lightly* with hair spray or clear acrylic spray.

## Hair

Various yarns, in interesting textures and shades, are ideal for doll hair. Blend two textures or shades of yarn for a special effect, but be sure to keep yarn in scale with the doll size.

Natural fibers such as cotton yarns, linen, twine, untwisted rope, and unspun wool can be used as hair for character dolls. For small dolls, use embroidery floss and crewel yarn.

To make yarn curls, wrap *acrylic* yarn tightly around *metal* knitting needles. Bake in a 350° oven for 5 to 10 minutes, then let the yarn cool and unwind the curls from the needle. *Note:* Because the size of the needles will determine the looseness of the curl, and some yarns will change color as they bake, always test the yarn and the needles first.

Make hair slightly longer than necessary so the ends can be trimmed evenly later. To attach hair to the head, "couch" yarn by sewing over it with matching thread, or use darning needles to stitch wig to doll.

## Clothing

If you are making your own clothing patterns, use the doll body as a guide for the size. The doll will help determine the sleeve and skirt lengths, the width of the bodice, and any other measurements needed. Add enough to the clothing dimensions so the garments fit over each other easily.

As you design the clothes, cut your patterns from paper towels. The towels are soft enough to drape and pleat, and they fold more easily than stiff paper. Tape the pieces together to visualize the finished garment. Be sure to add seam allowances before cutting out patterns.

For your doll's clothing, select fabrics that will not fray easily. Avoid bulky or flimsy fabrics and fabrics that wrinkle.

If you are making an old-fashioned doll, dip fabrics into a solution of strong, hot tea for an antique finish.

Be sure to keep the scale of prints, patterns, trims, and buttons in proportion to the size of the doll. Spot-glue trims in position before stitching if they are difficult to handle.

**Patterns:** In general, simple pattern shapes, based on squares, rectangles, or circles, are easiest to work with. Design the doll's clothing using as few pattern pieces as possible, relying on tucks, gathers, darts, and pleats for shaping garments to doll body.

It's easy to make patterns for many clothing items using a rectangle—skirts, sleeves, ruffles, a scarf, slip, apron, poncho, purse, bath towel, and even a ballerina's tutu.

For pants and panties, tape the raw edges of a square or rectangle to doll's center front and back. To form crotch, cut away small amounts at a time until shape fits to the body.

For bodice fronts and backs, use rectangles or squares. Tape the shapes to the doll, cutting away the armholes and necklines carefully.

Cut bibs for overalls or aprons, and hankies from squares. Use triangles for scarves or shawls.

With circles, create a nightcap, beret, carryall tote bag, and a full circular skirt. Use a half-circle to make a cape, cutting a half circle into center of the straight edge for an opening. To form a hooded cape, cut out an oval and run gathers or a casing strip across the width of the oval to create a hood. (Allow at least 1/3 of the oval for creating the hood.)

**Clothing construction:** When sewing clothing, try to stitch all of the seams by machine. If areas are too intricate for machine stitching, use tiny backstitches, stitching seams twice if necessary. This is very important if you are making removable clothing that small children will tug and stretch during playtime.

Small buttons or snaps, hooks and eyes, or ribbon or fabric ties are the best fastenings to use for easily removable doll clothing; zippers and nylon hook and loop fasteners tend to add unsightly bulk to the garment.

*For doll stockings,* use knitted infant stockings. Turn stocking inside out and slip onto doll's foot; position as desired. Pull stocking taut to the back and bottom of the doll foot and pin. Then remove the stocking from the doll's foot and stitch the back and bottom seam using the pins as a guide. Restitch the seam and trim the seam allowance close to the stitching. Turn stocking right side out.

*To make undergarments,* use fine cotton or handkerchief-weight fabric for panties, petticoats, slips, and chemises. To reduce bulk, eliminate as many of the seams as possible at the sides and shoulders by combining seam lines with the folds of the fabric.

*For shoes,* felt works well. Trace doll's foot onto paper for pattern, and add a 1/4-inch seam allowance.

Stiffen soles by inserting pieces of cardboard, cut slightly smaller than the soles. Use iron-on mending tape to add body to shoe pieces; add miniature straps, buckles, beads, or fringe to embellish the shoes.

*Fashion a stylish hat* from a tiny straw basket. Cut off the handle, turn basket upside down, and adorn with flowers and ribbon.

*For nearsighted dolls,* shape a pair of glasses from florist's wire; dip into plastic film (available in crafts stores.)

*For a doll umbrella,* use a Japanese paper parasol (sold in party shops) as a base. Carefully cover the form with lightweight fabric (use spray adhesive); trim with ruffles or lace.

*For doll jewelry,* collect junk jewelry and old buttons, as well as strings of tiny beads. Single earrings or antique buttons make wonderful brooches; and single pearl beads, or knots of glass beads make elegant earrings. Be sure to string the beads on sturdy thread, to avoid breakage.

Some final tips: Be on the lookout for small notions and odds and ends to add to your store of doll-making supplies. Stock up whenever and wherever you find them.

Study books on the history of fashion or design for costume ideas. If you are interested in authenticity, keep files on colors, fabrics, and accessories popular in different eras, and collect clippings or sketches from books and magazines.

# BROTHERS & SISTERS

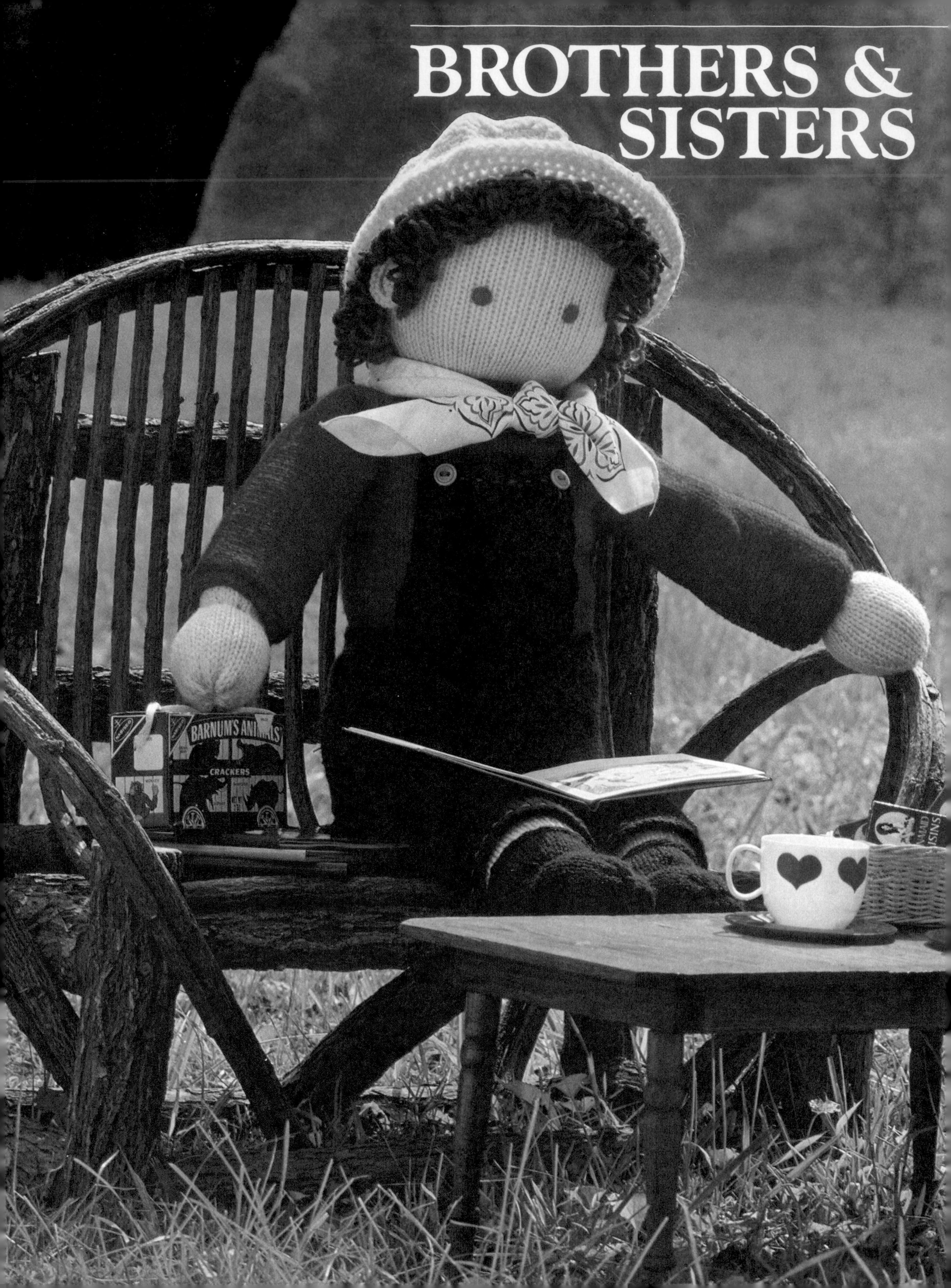

Like spring days and picnics, the brother and sister dolls in this chapter just naturally go together. From the child-size knitted pair shown here to the fabric and felt playmates on the next few pages, these dolls will be friends forever with the real little boys and girls who are lucky enough to receive them. For instructions, please turn the page.

# K·N·I·T·T·E·D  P·A·L·S

**W**hat better companions could a child have than two lovable friends to share tea with, read to, and take along on summer picnics? The life-size brother and sister dolls shown on pages 50 and 51 are the perfect pals, crafted with washable yarn and fiberfill stuffing that makes them so huggable, your child may never put them down.

And because they're constructed with one knitting stitch and just a touch of crochet, the dolls are easily made even by beginners.

### Abbreviations

| | |
|---|---|
| beg | begin(ning) |
| bet | between |
| ch | chain stitch |
| dc | double crochet |
| dec | decrease |
| hdc | half double crochet |
| inc | increase |
| k | knit |
| lp(s) | loop(s) |
| rem | remaining |
| rep | repeat |
| rnd | round |
| sc | single crochet |
| sk | skip |
| sl st | slip stitch |
| sp(s) | space(s) |
| st(s) | stitch(es) |
| st st | stockinette stitch |
| tog | together |
| * | repeat from * as indicated |
| ( ) | work directions given in parenthesis number of times specified |

### Materials for girl
- Bernat Berella-4 yarn in the following amounts and colors: 8 ounces of peach, 8 ounces of oyster white, 4 ounces of marsh heather
- 3 ounces of medium brown sport-weight yarn; 1 ounce of dark brown sport-weight yarn
- Black felt
- Polyester fiberfill
- ¼-inch-wide peach ribbon
- Size 6 knitting needles, or size to obtain gauge given below
- Size G crochet hook, or size to obtain gauge given below

**Gauge:** With knitting needles over st st, 4 sts = 1 inch. With crochet hook, 4 dc = 1 inch.

### Materials for boy
- Bernat Berella-4 in the following amounts and colors: 4 ounces of pale peach, 6 ounces of navy, 4 ounces of red, 1 ounce of white, 2 ounces of dark brown, 3 ounces of light brown, 3 ounces of yellow
- Polyester fiberfill
- Size 6 knitting needle, or size to obtain gauge given below
- Size G steel crochet hook, or size to obtain gauge given below.

**Gauge:** With knitting needles over st st, 4 sts = 1 inch. With crochet hook, 4 sc = 1 inch.

### Instructions
#### Knitted Girl Doll

**Body construction:** Beg at bottom of torso with white yarn (pantaloon hips), cast on 62 sts; work even in st st for 5 inches. Change to pale peach yarn (torso); continue even in st st for 18 inches.

*Next row:* K 2 tog across, cast off. Gather cast-off edge and darn the edge closed. Changing yarn colors to match work, sew side edges tog to form tube so that smooth side is right side. Stuff firmly so that tube is firm. Sew bottom closed.

**Arms:** Beg at hands with knitting needles and pale peach, cast on 32 sts. Work even in st st for 12 inches. Cast off as before. Darn cast-off edge closed and sew seam as before. Stuff firmly, leaving last inch unstuffed.

**Legs:** With knitting needles and dark brown yarn, cast on 32 sts and work even in st st for 5 inches. Change to white (pantaloon legs) and work even in st st for 9 inches. Cast off. Darn the dark brown edge closed; sew seam. Stuff legs firmly, leaving top inch unstuffed. Turn up half of the boot, so that the foot forms toes pointing forward.

Insert legs into the open end of body and sew the seam closed. (This creates a hip hinge so that the doll can sit upright.)

**Head:** With doubled pale peach yarn, sew running stitches about 7 inches below top of head. Draw up tightly so that neck measures 11 inches around. Sew closed.

Stitch arms to torso about 1 inch below neck. To make hands, gather arms about 3 inches from ends, making the wrists.

**Hair:** Cut a 15-inch-wide piece of cardboard. Wrap brown yarn around it about 100 times. Tie off each end. Sew to the head (down the middle), spreading yarn evenly along doll's head. Cut wisps for bangs.

To make two 7-inch braids, wrap brown yarn around the cardboard about 85 times. Cut yarn off cardboard at both ends, tie a strand of yarn around the middle of each 15-inch bundle, and fold the bundles in half. Tie to looped ends of hair covering head and braid.

Cut 2½-inch-diameter black felt circles and sew to face for eyes.

**Trim:** With a crochet hook, sl st around the body using white yarn where the body and hip section of the pantaloons meet. Rep around each leg, where the boot and pantaloons meet. Around each ankle, work (ch 3, sl st in next st).

**Clothing: Dress** *(make 2):* With knitting needles and marsh heather yarn, cast on 48 sts. Work even in st st for 13 inches.

**Sleeves:** Cast on 20 sts at beg of next two rows. Work even in st st for 5 inches. Cast off. Sew front to back at side seams and shoulders, leaving about 8 inches open at neck to fit over doll's head.

**Sleeve and hem:** Sc evenly around the sleeve and hem join last st to first with sl st.

*Rnd 2:* Ch 3, and work 2 more dc in same sp, * sk 2 sts, work 3 dc in next st. Rep from * around; join last dc to first with sl st.

*Rnd 3:* Ch 3, 2 dc in same sp, * 3 dc in next sp. Rep from * around. Fasten off. Rep with rem sleeve and dress hem. Thread the ribbon through the sleeves and the hem of the dress. Do not draw up; tie in bows.

**Neckline:** Work 1 rnd sc and 1 rnd dc shells as for hem and sleeves. Fasten off. Thread ribbon through sps. Put dress on doll; draw up neckline and tie into bow.

**Apron:** With knitting needles and white yarn, cast on 48 sts. Work even in st st for 7 inches, ending on the purl side; turn.

*Next row:* K 3 tog across—16 sts. Work even on rem sts for 4 inches. Cast off; do not cut yarn. With crochet hook, sc evenly around entire piece, inc at each corner to keep work flat.

*Next rnd:* Work 3 dc in every other sc. Sew bib of apron to dress. Ch around neck and fasten off at shoulders. With doubled strand of white yarn, ch 100; do not break yarn but sl st directly across apron at dec row; ch 100 from edge of apron. Fasten off.

Tie 100-ch lengths into a bow at the back of the dress.

**Cap:** With crochet hook and white, ch 4, join and work 2 sts in each st until there are 24 sts. Work 1 rnd even.

*Next rnd:* Inc 1 st every 3rd st. Work 1 rnd even.

*Following rnd:* Inc 1 st every 4th st. Work 1 rnd even. Continue to alternate inc and even rnds until there are 136 sts in circle. Work 3 rnds even. Dec 1 st every 5 sts in next 3 rnds. Work 2 rnds even. Work 3 dc in every other st.

*Next rnd:* Work (3 dc, ch 1, 3 dc) in sps bet dc shells of previous rnd.

*Last rnd:* Work 3 dc in sps bet dc shells of previous rnd. Thread ribbon through first shell rnd of cap. Place hat on doll's head and gather slightly to fit. Tie ribbon in bow. Tack hat to hair of doll's head with white yarn.

## Instructions
### Knitted Boy Doll

**Body construction: Body and head:** Work same as for girl doll.

**Arms:** Work same as for girl doll.

**Legs:** Work dark brown shoes as for girl doll, k rem in pale peach.

Assemble, sew, and stuff as directed for the girl doll.

**Clothing: Overalls:** With knitting needles and navy, cast on 40 sts for waist of pant and work even in st st for 7 inches.

**Crotch shaping:** Cast on 2 sts at beg of next 2 rows. Work even in st st for 9 inches. Cast off.

With smooth sides facing and the crotch shapings matched, sew pants tog along crotch curves to the waist. Fold pants so seams meet; sew the inner leg seams.

**Bib:** Cast on 18 sts and work even in st st for 4 inches. Cast off. With crochet hook, work 2 rnds sc around top edge (waist) of pants; work 2 rnds sc around bib, then center bib to front of pants and sew to waist.

**Sweater:** With knitting needles and red, cast on 40 sts and work even in st st for 8 inches. Cast on 30 sts at beg of next 2 rows—100 sts. Work

even in st st for 4 inches. Cast off. Make another piece to match. Sew tog at side seams and undersleeve seams. Sew tog at shoulders, leaving 6 inches open for neck. With crochet hook, work 2 rnds sc around each cuff and 3 rnds around neck edge. Put sweater on doll and sew hem edge to body. Put overalls on doll, with bib to front, and sew waist and bib edges to sweater (overalls cover sweater hem edge). With doubled strand of navy yarn, ch from each top corner of bib, over the shoulder, and to the opposite side of waistband. (Straps cross in back.) Fasten off.

**Hat:** With crochet hook and yellow, ch 4; join with sl st to form ring. Work in rnds, making 2 sc in each sc, until there are 24 sts in rnd. *Next and every other rnd:* Work even. *Inc rnds* (every other rnd): Make an inc every 2nd st for first inc rnd, an inc every 3rd st for 2nd inc rnd, an inc every 4th st for 3rd inc rnd, etc. Rep inc rnd until there are 60 sts in rnd. Work 9 rnds even. Change to red and work 2 rnds even.

**Brim:** Attach yellow and inc once every 6th st. *Next and every other rnd:* Work even. *Inc rnds* (every other rnd): Make an inc in every 7th st for next inc rnd, an inc in every 8th st for following inc rnd, then an inc in every 9th st for final inc rnd. Fasten off. Crimp crown of hat; tack in place.

**Hair:** With light brown yarn and yarn needle, cover back and sides of hair with 2-inch lps, following each lp with a staystitch so that hair does not fall out (turkey-work stitch).

**Ears:** With crochet hook and pale peach, ch 4; join. Work in rnds, making 2 sc in each sc, until there are a total of 20 sts.

*Next rnd:* Work hdc in each of first 2 sts, 2 dc in next st, hdc in each of next 2 sts, sl st in next st. Fasten off, leaving a tail for sewing. Sew ears to head, then pull hat on head with crimp facing front. Tack hat to head.

# F·E·L·T  F·R·I·E·N·D·S

**A**s soft to the touch as a favorite blanket, these felt playmates are ideal for toddlers. Just for fun, select other fabrics and accessories and fashion the dolls' outfits after your children's own playclothes.

## Materials

- ¼ yard of flesh-colored felt
- Gray, white, blue, and green felt scraps (shoes, eyes, hat)
- ¼ yard of striped knit fabric (shirt)
- ¼ yard of blue fabric (pants)
- ¼ yard of red polka-dot fabric (dress, bloomers)
- ¼ yard of white cotton fabric (pinafore)
- Carbon paper; typing paper
- 2 yards of narrow white rickrack
- Brown crewel yarn (hair)
- Pink embroidery floss
- Powdered rouge; narrow elastic
- White sewing thread; snaps
- White glue

## Instructions

Enlarge patterns, *opposite,* onto typing paper; cut out. Trace and cut each pattern piece from fabric. Patterns include ³⁄₁₆ inch for seam allowances.

**Body construction: Head:** For eyes, cut two white felt circles and two blue felt circles (slightly smaller than the white circles) for each doll. Glue the eyes in place, centering the blue felt on top of the white felt. Outline-stitch the nose and mouth using pink floss. Color the cheeks with rouge.

Stitch ears together, leaving the straight edge open; stuff lightly. (Do not turn right side out.) Repeat procedure to make a total of four ears (two for each doll). Baste ears in place.

With right sides facing, stitch front and back head pieces together, leaving the top edge open. Clip curves, turn right side out, stuff, and slip-stitch the opening closed.

**Body:** With right sides facing, stitch front and back body pieces together, leaving the bottom edge open. Clip curves and turn right side out (do not stuff). Tack back of head (along the bottom) to center of neck.

**Legs:** With right sides facing, stitch shoes to bottom of each leg. With right sides facing, stitch front and back leg pieces together, leaving top and bottom edges open. (Make four legs—two for each doll.)

Slip-stitch a sole to the bottom of each shoe. Clip curves, turn, and stuff, leaving 1 inch at the top of each leg unstuffed. Baste legs in place to front body piece; baste and stitch seat to bottom edge of body along front. Stuff; slip-stitch opening closed.

**Arms:** With right sides facing, stitch arm pieces together, leaving top and bottom (fingers) open. (Make four arms—two for each doll.) Clip curves and turn. Work tiny overcast stitches around edge of each thumb and finger. Stuff arms; slip-stitch opening closed. Tack arms in place to body.

**Clothing: Dress:** Stitch the raglan sleeves to the front and back dress pieces; clip curves and press. Cut back of dress from neck to waist for neck opening (center seam); hem.

Hem sleeves and neck, gathering neck to 6½ inches and sleeves to 4 inches. Stitch dress and sleeve side seams. Hem dress. Use a snap to fasten dress at neck.

**Pinafore:** Cut back pinafore piece to make a neck opening; hem the edges. Stitch front and back pieces together at shoulder seams. Trim the hem, neck, and armholes with narrow white rickrack. Sew pocket to pinafore front; stitch both side seams. Use a snap to fasten pinafore at neck.

**Bloomers:** Cut bloomers and hem each leg. With right sides facing, sew front and back pieces together along front and back seams. Stitch a casing in the top edge of the bloomers and insert narrow elastic.

**Shirt:** Cut a small slit in the back of the shirt at the neck; hem edges and stitch a snap in place. Stitch the front

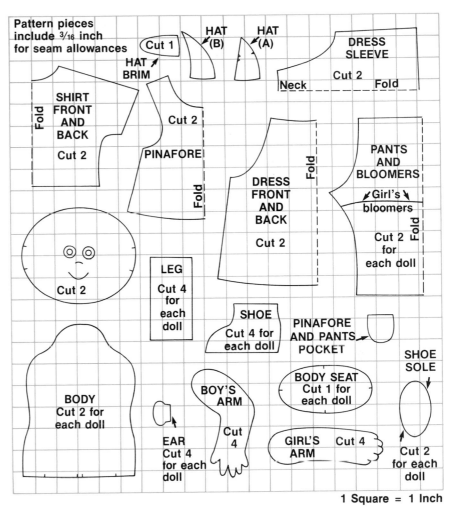

1 Square = 1 Inch

and the back pieces together at the shoulders. Hem the neck and the sleeves. Sew the side and the under sleeves. Press under hem at the bottom of the shirt, and stitch.

**Pants:** Hem the bottom of each pant leg. Stitch two hip pockets in place to the back of the pants. Stitch the front center seam and the back center seam; stitch the leg and side seams. Turn and stitch a hem across the top of the pants.

**Hat:** Cut two blue A pieces and two green A pieces from felt; cut two blue B pieces and two green B pieces from felt. Stitch identical front and back hat pieces by sewing the A and B pieces together, alternating colors and A/B pieces. With right sides facing, stitch the front and back hat pieces together, leaving the bottom edge open. Turn right side out and stuff lightly.

Stitch the hat in place to the top of the boy's head, turning under raw edges and inserting brim on one side.

**Hair: Boy:** Use brown crewel 3-ply yarn, and stitch randomly placed straight stitches along the bottom of the hat around the sides and the back of the head.

**Girl:** Wrap the brown crewel yarn around a 1-inch-wide ruler for about 4 inches. Using a zipper foot, stitch along one side; slide yarn off the ruler. Stitch the loops to the top of the head (across the top) for bangs.

Wrap brown crewel yarn around a 3x6-inch piece of cardboard. Remove yarn from cardboard and stitch each loop in place across the back of the head. Draw up each yarn loop and tack in place to make a "Dutch bob" hairdo.

# L·I·T·T·L·E  L·E·A·G·U·E·R·S

**S**titched up in the colors of your home team, these dolls will be winners with every baseball fan in town! The fabric-and-felt uniforms are designed with detail, but they're simple to sew. Best of all, they're delightfully authentic—right down to the catcher's mitts, spats, and sporty laced-up shoes.

## Materials

- ¾ yard *each* of 45-inch-wide flesh-colored and light pink fabric
- ⅓ yard *each* of 45-inch-wide blue-and-white and red-and-white pinstripe fabric
- Scraps of yellow, green, and white T-shirt knit
- Scraps of yellow, green, red, navy, white, tan, and brown felt
- Red and navy fabrics and T-shirt tube-style ribbing
- Green, red, blue, and yellow grosgrain ribbons; interfacing
- Red, brown, pink, orange, white, and blue embroidery floss
- Reddish-brown and dark-brown knitting worsted-weight yarn
- Two ⁹⁄₁₆-inch-diameter self-covered buttons; snaps
- Polyester fiberfill
- Powdered rouge
- Dressmaker's carbon paper

## Instructions

Finished size is 21 inches tall.

Enlarge the patterns, *page 58*. The patterns include ¼ inch for seam allowances. Double-stitch all of the seams for added strength. Stitch the pieces together with right sides facing unless noted otherwise. Use three strands of floss for embroidery.

**Doll body: Head:** Transfer head patterns to fabric (flesh-colored for boy, pink for girl); transfer face pattern to right side of one head piece.

*Girl's face:* Cut out two brown felt eye pieces. Whipstitch eyes to face. Outline-stitch around the eyes and straight-stitch the eyelashes using brown floss. Add white eye accents. Use brown French knots for freckles. Outline-stitch the eyebrows with one strand of brown floss. Outline-stitch a pink nose and red mouth; straight-stitch corners of the mouth with red. Brush the cheeks, chin, and nose with powdered rouge, using dotted lines on pattern as a guide.

*Boy's face:* Embroider as directed for girl, except work nose and mouth with orange and eliminate eyebrows.

Cut out head patterns; stitch darts and press. Stitch face to head back. Clip curves; turn and stuff firmly.

**Body:** Cut the body, arms, legs, and sole pieces from flesh-colored fabric for boy, and pink fabric for girl.

Stitch body side seams and bottom seam, leaving neck open. Turn; stuff firmly. Turn neck facing to the inside. Insert head into opening; blindstitch head to body, adding more stuffing as needed. (Refer to page 23 for tips on stuffing dolls.)

**Arms:** Stitch arms together, leaving tops open. Restitch thumb areas. Clip curves. Trim seam allowances to ⅛ inch. Turn. Stuff hands moderately and stuff arms firmly to within ¾ inch of the top. Whipstitch the openings closed. Backstitch lines for fingers. Stitch arms to body.

**Legs:** Stitch center front and center back seams of legs, leaving tops and soles open. Clip curves and press seams. Stitch one sole to each leg, matching center fronts and backs. Clip curves, turn, and stuff firmly to within ¾ inch of the tops. Whipstitch the openings closed; stitch the legs to the body.

**Hair:** *For the boy's bangs and hair,* tack down a length of reddish-brown yarn at top seam of head. Using a continuous strand of yarn, embroider turkey work stitches along the front and sides of face, making loops as long as the length of the bangs (use the pattern as a guide). Tack center of each loop to fabric.

Stitch two additional rows of turkey work on top of first loops. *Note:* Repeat procedure for back of head, making each row shorter than the preceding row to give hair height.

*Girl's hair:* Using brown yarn, make hair as directed above for boy. To make braids, wrap yarn 30 times around an 11-inch length of cardboard. Secure at one end; cut opposite end. Divide yarn into three equal parts and braid. Tack to side of head with yarn. Repeat for other braid. Trim ends of braids, then add bows.

**Clothing: Stockings:** Cut pattern pieces from white knit fabric. Stitch center back seams, using a ⅛-inch seam. Turn tops under ¼ inch; press and hem.

**Spats:** Cut spat pieces from felt (yellow for girl, green for boy). Stitch the center back seam and the underfoot seam.

**Shoes:** Cut sole pieces and top pieces from felt (red for girl, navy for boy). Cut design pieces from white felt. For each top piece, topstitch along the lines indicated on pattern. Slip-stitch design pieces in place. Stitch the laces (see diagram) with floss, leaving a 3-inch tail at each end. Tie tails into bows; knot ends.

Stitch center back seam of each shoe top. Stitch tops to soles, using a ⅛-inch seam.

**Shirt:** From pinstripe fabric (blue-and-white for boy, red-and-white for girl), cut front and back pieces and sleeve pieces. Cut the lower T-shirt pieces from knit fabric (yellow for girl, green for boy).

Press under ¼ inch of center back edges; stitch. Cut numeral from felt (green for boy, yellow for girl); appliqué to shirt front. Stitch shirt front to back at shoulders; press seams.

For neck edge, cut a 1x9¼-inch piece of the T-shirt tube-style ribbing (blue for boy, red for girl). Fold in half lengthwise and stitch seams at each short end. Turn and press.

Stitch ribbing to neck, matching centers and raw edges. Zigzag-stitch raw edges; press to the inside.

Stitch ⅜-inch-wide grosgrain ribbon around pinstripe sleeve (green for boy, yellow for girl). Cut a 1x6-inch piece of ribbing for each sleeve. Fold in half lengthwise; press. Stitch the ribbing to the lower edge of pinstripe sleeve. Zigzag-stitch raw edges. Zigzag-stitch T-shirt sleeve to ribbing.

Stitch sleeves to shirt. Stitch shirt front to backs at sides and sleeves; press seams open. Press ¼ inch of the shirt bottom to the inside twice, and hem. Press the back facings to the inside of the shirt and slip-stitch to the hems. Turn ¼ inch of the T-shirt sleeves to the inside and hem. Sew snaps at back center.

**Trousers:** Cut the front and back pieces from pinstripe. Stitch center front seam. Clip curves; press seam open. Repeat for back pieces.

Stitch front to back at sides and inseam. Turn ¼ inch of the legs to the inside twice and hem. Machine-baste ¼ inch from upper edge of waist and gather. For waistband, cut a 1½x9½-inch piece of ribbing. Stitch short ends together to form a circle using a ⅛-inch seam. Wrong sides facing, fold ribbing in half; press and baste raw edges together. Stitch ribbing to trousers. Zigzag-stitch raw edge.

**Cap:** Cut brims, brim interfacings, crown X pieces, and crown Z pieces (blue fabric for boy, red for girl).

Stack and pin together the following: one brim interfacing, two brim pieces with right sides together, and another brim interfacing. Sew, leaving open between Xs. Trim seams, clip curves, turn and press. Topstitch brim along dashed lines.

Stitch two pairs of crown X pieces together from A to B. Clip curves; press seams open. Stitch pairs together along one A-B line. Stitch two pairs of crown Z pieces together from A to C. Clip curves; press seams open. Stitch crown Z pieces together *(continued)*

# Little Leaguers

*(continued)*

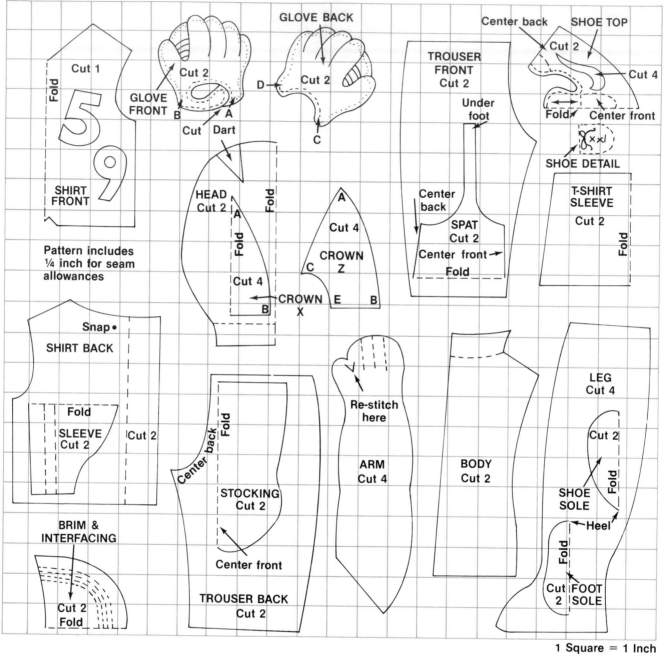

1 Square = 1 Inch

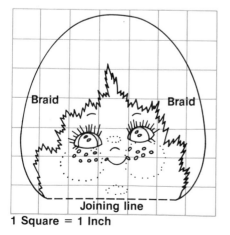

1 Square = 1 Inch

around curve from E to E. Trim seam, clip curves, turn, and press. Stitch crown X pieces to crown Z pieces from A to B. Clip curves; press the seams open. Stitch brim to crown, so that crown Z pieces are in the back.

Stitch a 14½-inch length of blue or red ¾-inch-wide grosgrain ribbon to inside of cap, overlapping 1 inch at front and leaving a 2-inch length of ribbon across the E to E opening. Stitch the ribbon to the seam allowance ⅛ inch away from the hem. Press ribbon to inside of cap. Cover button; stitch to center of crown.

**Gloves:** Cut gloves from tan felt. Stitch two front pieces together with wrong sides facing. Stitch the finger detail and from A to B using dark brown thread. With wrong sides facing, stitch two back pieces together. Stitch the finger detail and from C to D using dark brown thread. Stuff fingers of the front and back pieces. Pin the fronts to the backs and stitch outer edges from A-D around the fingertips to C-B as shown with the dotted lines on the pattern. Trim outer edges.

# Y·A·R·N   D·O·L·L·S

**Feet (or shoes):** From pink or navy blue fabric, cut two 3x3½-inch ovals for feet (shoes). Stitch together, following the hand instructions, *above*. Tack center tops of the feet (shoes) to the legs.

**Head:** Cut two 7-inch circles from pink jersey for each head. With right sides facing, sew the head pieces together, leaving neck open. Turn, slip head onto pink yarn, and stuff with fiberfill. Turn raw edges under and sew the neck to the yarn, securing the head to the body.

With a darning needle and strong thread, stitch button eyes into place, starting at the back of the head and sewing through the entire thickness of the doll's head.

Embroider mouth and eyebrows, using red and black floss. Sew a red pompon in place for the nose. Accent eyes with circles of white felt tacked behind the buttons.

**Hair:** Make wig bases from 6x7-inch ovals of brown or yellow felt. Cut several darts in front of ovals; stitch darts so felt curves to fit head.

Cut brown and yellow yarn into 3- and 4-inch pieces. Fold each piece of yarn in half; sew yarn to felt, alternating 3- and 4-inch lengths. Fill felt with rows of yarn, spacing rows ¼ inch apart. Leave ⅜ inch of felt around edges for attaching wig to head.

Cut twelve 8-inch pieces of yellow yarn, fold each piece in half, and sew six pieces to each side of the girl doll's face. Tie strands with red bows. Stitch wigs to heads, and trim.

**Ears:** Cut four 1x1½-inch ovals for *each* doll from pink jersey. Sew two ears together, leaving an opening. Turn, sew opening, and tack to head.

**Clothing:** Make simple clothing for the dolls by sewing together squares and rectangles for shirt or blouse, pants, and skirt. *Note:* For design ideas and special construction tips, see pages 46 to 49.

**W**ith their soft yarn bodies and simple clothes, these sweet dolls are perfect gifts for infants. (For safety, replace button eyes with felt.) Or craft them in large quantities for bazaars — their touchable texture makes them best sellers!

## Materials
**(for two dolls)**
- 3 skeins of pink craft yarn
- ¼ yard of pink jersey
- 1 skein *each* of brown and yellow 4-ply yarn
- 7x8 inches *each* of brown and yellow felt; white felt
- Four ¾-inch black buttons
- 2 red pompons
- Black and red embroidery floss
- Fiberfill; darning needle
- 13x18-inch piece of cardboard

## Instructions
**Body:** Cut eight 10-inch pieces of pink yarn; wind remaining yarn from the skein parallel to the 18-inch side of the cardboard to create the body. Tie both ends with 10-inch pieces of yarn; slip yarn off cardboard. Tie off section for head 4 inches from top.

Wind second skein of pink yarn 50 times around the cardboard (parallel to the 13-inch side of the cardboard) for arms. Tie the two ends securely; slip yarn off card. Slip arms through body, tie off at waist. Untie piece at bottom of body; divide yarn in half. Tie each with a 10-inch yarn length.

**Hands:** Draw a hand pattern approximately 3 inches long from wrist to fingertips and 3 inches across at its widest point. Cut four hands for each doll from pink jersey. With right sides facing, sew two hand pieces together, using a ¼-inch seam; leave wrist open. Clip seams; turn and stuff. Turn raw edges under; sew hand to arm, covering yarn tie.

# H·O·M·E·B·O·D·Y  T·W·I·N·S

**H**igh-button shoes, thick red hair, and charming old-fashioned clothes aren't all these homebodies have in common. They're twins in the truest sense of the word because they're both made from one simple pattern.

## Materials
**(for both dolls)**
- 1¼ yards of 45-inch-wide muslin
- ½ yard (45 inches wide) *each* of green polka-dot, green print, brown corduroy, green gingham, rust, and brown fabrics
- Thread to match fabrics
- Blue, rust, coral, and pale yellow embroidery floss
- Buttons as follows: Four ⅜-inch-diameter gold, one ½-inch-diameter green, ten ⅜-inch-diameter black, ten ⅜-inch-diameter pearl
- 2 yards of ivory rickrack
- 1¼ yards of 1-inch-wide ivory eyelet
- 1 yard of ½-inch braid
- 1 yard of ⅜-inch-wide ribbon
- 1½ yards of ¼-inch elastic
- Snaps; bias tape
- 1 pound of polyester fiberfill
- 1 skein *each* of rust and orange rug yarn

## Instructions
Finished size is 24 inches.

Enlarge patterns (bodies are the same for both dolls) onto tissue paper and cut out. All pattern pieces include ¼-inch seam allowances.

**Body (for both dolls):** Transfer body pattern and face details onto muslin. Do not cut out.

Satin-stitch blue eyes and coral mouths; outline-stitch yellow nose, and rust eyebrows and eyelids. Cut out body pieces.

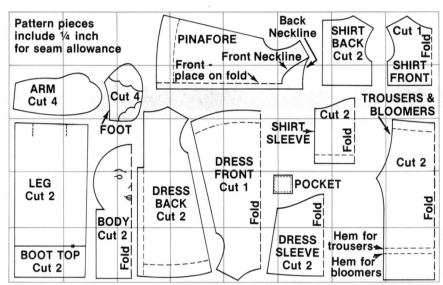

1 Square = 2 Inches

With right sides facing, sew body front to back; leave open body base and armhole space. Turn; press.

**Arms:** Stitch arms, leaving opening for turning. Turn and press.

**Feet (boots) and legs:** Zigzag machine-stitch brown heel and toe designs onto rust boots, following foot pattern. Sew boot top to foot. Stitch boot to leg. With right sides facing, stitch around each leg/boot piece, leaving top open. Turn, press, and stuff. Sew buttons to sides of boots.

Stuff doll arms; stitch to body. Stuff head and body. Stitch legs to front of body; turn under back seam and slip-stitch closed.

**Hair: For girl:** Smooth out skein of rust yarn into a 7½-inch-wide strip. Place masking tape widthwise across center of yarn; stitch through yarn and tape. Remove tape; slip-stitch wig to head. Tie the hair into ponytails; add bows, trim yarn, and tack to head.

**For boy:** Thread a single strand of orange yarn double in a large needle. Beginning at the base of the hairline, stitch the hair to the back of the boy doll's head by making 2-inch-long rya knots in evenly spaced rows, every ½ inch up to top of head. On front of doll, stitch from ear line around front, following seam line. Clip loops; trim hair.

**Clothing for the girl: Bloomers:** Cut bloomers from muslin; stitch seams. Add two rows of eyelet trim. Turn under top edge for casing. Insert elastic; trim to fit. Stitch casing closed.

**Dress:** Cut dress from polka-dot fabric. Stitch back seam up to back opening. Stitch front to back at shoulders. Gather sleeve top; stitch to dress. Hem sleeves; stitch band of elastic ½ inch from bottom of sleeve; fit to doll arm. Stitch side and sleeve seams. Hem dress; finish neck edge with bias tape. Add snap closings.

**Pinafore:** Cut pinafore from print. Sew side and shoulder seams. Turn up hem. Finish bottom edge, back edges, neckline, and armholes with rickrack. Fasten with green button and buttonhole in back. Stitch pocket in place; add hankie.

**Clothing for the boy: Trousers:** Cut trousers from brown corduroy; stitch as for bloomers, omitting eyelet. Turn up 3-inch hem; turn back to form cuffs. Cut two pieces of braid (suspenders). Cross in back and tack in place. Sew gold buttons in place.

**Shirt:** Stitch shoulder seams and insert sleeves; stitch the side and the sleeve seams. Hem sleeve edge. Finish the neck edge with bias tape. Cut scarf from scrap fabric.

# P·A·T·C·H·W·O·R·K  P·L·A·Y·M·A·T·E·S

## TO MACHINE-APPLIQUÉ

Young children are bound to be pleased with this fanciful two-some. But don't be surprised if their not-so-small siblings request these dolls for their own rooms, too!

We used fabric appliqués to make our pair, but there are other options. Decorate the dolls with fabric crayons or pencils, and let your kids lend a helping hand. Then, just sew the dolls together and stuff.

You can stitch them knee-high as shown here, or make them kid-size, and bring the dolls "to life."

## Materials
**(for each doll)**
- ⅔ yard of black cotton fabric (background and backing)
- Assorted fabric scraps (appliqués)
- ½ yard of 18-inch-wide fusible webbing
- Muslin scrap (face and hands)
- Kraft paper
- Tissue paper
- Matching thread
- Polyester fiberfill
- Dressmaker's carbon paper
- Yarn (girl's hair)
- Pearl buttons, satin ribbons, and other trims
- Powdered rouge or fabric paints (cheeks)

## Instructions
*Note:* The doll fronts are constructed from machine-appliquéd fabric. The fabric appliqués are cut *without* seam allowances and fused onto a black fabric background. They fit together like jigsaw puzzle pieces.

After the raw edges are machine-appliquéd with zigzag satin stitches, the doll fronts and plain fabric backs are stitched together, stuffed with polyester fiberfill, and finished with three-dimensional details such as buttons, yarn hair, and ribbon bows.

**Creating patterns:** Enlarge the doll patterns, *below,* onto Kraft paper to make master patterns.

*Note:* Make smaller or larger dolls by simply changing the scale on the diagram (1 square equals 3 inches, 1 square equals 1 inch, and so forth.)

Place tissue paper on top of the master patterns and trace around each shape to form the individual pattern pieces for appliqué work.

Add a 3-inch margin to the master pattern outline.

For one doll, cut two black fabric pieces to match the enlarged outline of the doll (one for the front and one for the back).

**Appliquéing the dolls:** Transfer the outlines onto the front pattern piece using white dressmaker's carbon paper. This will serve as a guide for positioning appliqués.

For the doll front, cut appliqué pieces from tissue patterns beginning with pieces at the doll base and working toward the head.

**For the girl:** Cut shoe base, shoe highlights, stockings, and collar from white fabric. From muslin, cut legs, arms, and face. From yellow fabric, cut skirt, sleeve, and collar trims.

**For the boy:** Cut stockings from baby blue fabric, knickers from pale green, shirt from white, tie from black and white checked fabric, and a small marble from a scrap of red fabric. Cut hands and face from muslin.

Cut matching pieces from fusible webbing. Lay fabric appliqués and fusible webbing into place on the front background piece. Fuse in place using an iron.

Transfer facial details and all clothing detail lines onto appliqués using dressmaker's carbon paper.

Machine-appliqué around all raw edges, using machine satin stitches and thread to match fabric. Machine-embroider facial details with close, short zigzag stitches in dark thread.

1 Square = 1½ Inches

Zigzag-stitch the girl's collar, cuffs, and skirt trim details with black thread for contrast.

For the boy doll, zigzag-stitch inner details on shirt and knickers using navy blue thread.

With right sides facing, pin appliquéd doll front to backing fabric; sew together 1 inch from raw edges, leaving an opening along a straight edge for turning. Trim seams and clip the curves very evenly.

Turn doll to the right side; stuff firmly with polyester fiberfill and slip-stitch the opening closed.

**Finishing the dolls: For the girl:** Cut two 2½x36-inch strips from red pin-dot and red checked fabric. With right sides facing, stitch strips together along long edges. Trim seams, and turn to right side. Tie into hair bow and trim ends, leaving raw edges exposed on the short ends, or turning the edges under and slip-stitching them closed. Tack bow to head.

Sew three pearl buttons to front of dress. Tie bows from black satin ribbon and tack to shoes. Glue or slip-stitch lengths of yarn to head for hair.

Brush the cheeks with powdered rouge, or paint with fabric paints.

**For the boy:** Draw stocking details onto fabric using gray or black permanent fine-tip marking pens.

*Note:* There are many other crafting techniques that may be used to decorate these dolls. Fabric paints, fabric crayons, felt pens, colored pencils, embroidery stitches, quilting, trapunto, or a combination of several of these embellishments, all work well for decorating the dolls. See pages 76 to 79 for specific instructions.

# FANCIFUL DOLLS
## WITH SPECIAL USES

Function and fantasy go hand in hand to make the dolls in this chapter refreshingly different. Beginning with this bridal party crafted of spoons, you'll find an old-world maiden who doubles as a tea cozy, a storybook pal who's also a pajama bag, and other dolls that are every bit as practical as they are fun to make.

# P·A·R·T·Y  F·A·V·O·R·S

**I**magination is just about all you need to make the dolls shown on pages 64 and 65. Use these mementos as a centerpiece (ours are for a bridal shower), and distribute them as favors when the festivities are done.

## Materials

- 12- to 13-inch spoon (large doll)
- 6½-inch spoon (small doll)
- 6 long pipe cleaners (large doll)
- 2 long pipe cleaners (small doll)
- 22 inches of white cotton cable cord, size 400 (large doll)
- Scraps of fabrics, laces, ribbons (clothing), and knit fabric (hands)
- Acrylic paints
- Polyurethane
- Black, fine-point, marking pen
- Tissue paper
- Carbon paper

**Full-size features**

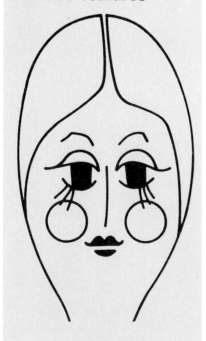

## Instructions

**Large dolls: Faces:** Draw faces on curved side of spoons with a pencil. Or, transfer the full-size pattern, *below left,* onto spoon, using carbon paper.

Outline facial features with a permanent felt marker. Paint eyes and lips with acrylic paints; allow to dry. Coat face with polyurethane.

Enlarge patterns, *below right,* onto tissue paper; cut out.

**Body: Arms:** Twist three pipe cleaners together; bend one end into a loop to form a hand. Twist opposite end around spoon handle neck, leaving a 5-inch length of pipe cleaner for arm. Repeat for second arm.

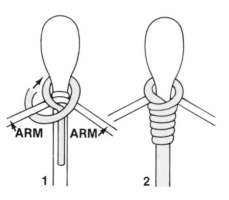

**Hands:** Draw around the hand pattern on double thickness of knit fabric. Sew on drawn lines, leaving opening for turning; cut out hands. Turn to right side; slip over pipe-cleaner hands.

**Upper body:** Tape each end of the cotton cord to prevent raveling. Following diagram, *above,* wrap cording around handle, crisscrossing over the arms and wrapping down the handle. Secure cord.

**Clothing: Dress bodice:** Cut bodice pattern from fabric. Turn under raw edges of sleeve. Stitch front and back together along the sides and sleeves. Turn; slip dress onto doll, turn under raw edge of back opening, and slipstitch back closed. Run a gathering thread around bottom edge of sleeve and pull tightly around arm. Secure the thread. Sew lace trim around neck. Add additional trims, if desired.

**Skirt:** Cut a 10-inch-wide piece of fabric long enough to cover spoon handle, plus a hem allowance. Sew up back seam; hem skirt. Run a gathering thread around top edge. Slip skirt onto doll, pulling gathers to fit. Adjust gathers and whipstitch skirt to doll, catching bodice in the stitching. Tie ribbon or lace apron around waist to conceal raw edges. Add lace trims.

**For smaller dolls:** Proceed as directed, *above,* following the exceptions given, *below.*

**Arms:** Twist two long pipe cleaners together. Bend loops on both ends for hands. Make a loop large enough to go around handle, in center of pipe cleaner. Slip handle into loop; push loop up as far as possible. Glue.

**Dress:** Cut pattern from fabric. Hem sleeves. Stitch front and back together; turn and press. Place the dress on the doll. Gather neck opening and secure. Add lace and other trims.

**For bride doll:** Construct as for larger dolls, with exceptions, *below.*

**Gown:** Cut skirt 15 inches wide and the length of the handle. Tack pearls and lace flowers to skirt.

**Veil:** Cut 18x24 inches of netting. Trim with lace. Run gathering thread 1½ inches from top. Gather lace to measure 3 inches; secure. Glue veil to spoon, fanning net toward face.

**Accessories:** Add seed pearl earrings and flowers to hair. Make a bouquet from paper flowers, "framing" them with a doily; add ribbons.

Pattern pieces include ⅛ inch for seam allowances.

1 Square = 1 Inch

# T·E·A - C·O·Z·Y  H·O·S·T·E·S·S

**T**his mischievous maiden is a cheerful companion who secretly doubles as a kitchen helper. Her richly colored old-world costume hides a double layer of fiberfill to keep your teapot warm.

Machine stitchery makes the crafting quick and easy. So why not make this merry cozy for yourself, then stitch another as a perfect housewarming or wedding gift? And if your children are too enchanted to leave her in the kitchen, surprise them with a playtime version of their very own.

For the pattern and instructions for this doll, please turn the page.

## Tea-Cozy Hostess

*(continued)*

### Materials

- 22x32 inches of 1½-inch-thick quilt batting
- ¼ pound of polyester fiberfill
- 1 yard *each* of 45-inch-wide muslin and ecru woven fabric
- 13x45 inches of striped fabric
- 10x10x18-inch kerchief triangle
- ⅛ yard of black fabric
- 1½ yards of 2-inch-wide lace
- 1 yard of 2-inch-wide embroidered trim
- ¾ yard of ecru bias tape
- 8 grommets
- Black yarn
- Black, blue, and red embroidery floss
- Thread to match fabrics

### Instructions

Finished size is 18 inches tall.

**Cozy:** Cut one 22x32-inch rectangle from muslin. Fold the muslin in half lengthwise.

Lightly mark quilting lines with pencil as follows: Draw one horizontal line 2 inches from the folded edge; from this line, draw perpendicular, vertical lines spaced at 2-inch intervals. Extend them to the raw edge.

Unfold muslin and place atop batting; baste together.

Refold cozy, with batting sides together. Machine-quilt along all lines. Roll ends of cozy together to form 11-inch-high tube; blindstitch ends together. Machine-quilt over seam.

For casing, cut one 2½x32-inch muslin strip; sew short ends together.

With right sides together, sew strip to top of cozy. Fold in half (turning under raw edge), and slip-stitch to inside of cozy. Run a gathering thread through the casing.

**Body:** Enlarge the pattern, *opposite,* onto brown paper.

Transfer the face pattern onto muslin using dressmaker's carbon paper. *Do not cut out pattern.*

With fabric in a hoop, embroider the face with three strands of floss. Work red outline stitches for the mouth, blue satin stitches for eyes, and black outline stitches for remaining features. Cut out all patterns.

With right sides facing, sew the chin to the face between large Xs.

Sew dart on body front, then sew neck and body front together between small Xs. Sew center back seam on back upper body.

With right sides facing, sew the body front to the back, fitting and easing curves around the head and the shoulders. Leave the bottom of the body open. Clip the curves wherever necessary. Stuff the body firmly with fiberfill. Turn under the raw edges and slip-stitch the opening closed.

Stitch around the arms, leaving the tops open. Stuff with polyester fiberfill and set aside.

**Hair:** Cut thirty 40-inch lengths of black yarn. Center the lengths at top of forehead and tack the strands in place—along the hairline and around the face. (Do not sew yarn to back of head unless desired—the kerchief will cover the back of the head.)

Fashion the ends of the yarn into buns at each side of the face.

Tie triangular kerchief around head and tack in several places.

**Clothing:** Cut one 6x16-inch rectangle (blouse), two 14-inch squares (sleeves), and one 11-inch square (apron) from ecru fabric.

**Blouse:** Gather the blouse rectangle along one long edge. Sew 2-inch trim onto one edge of each sleeve and apron. Add lace at the sleeve and apron edges.

Put blouse on upper body of doll, gathering the neck to fit. Tack blouse to doll at center back and cover raw edge at neck with lace trim.

Sew underarm seams on sleeves, run a gathering thread along sleeve tops, and slip sleeves over the arms.

Gather sleeves to fit shoulders. Tuck raw edges under and slip-stitch sleeve tops to doll. Gather sleeves above trim and tack to lower arms.

Gather cozy to fit around bottom of upper body; pin in place. Slip-stitch to upper body.

**Apron:** Finish apron edges, and gather top to 7 inches wide. Sew bias tape over gathers to make waistband and set apron aside.

**Vest:** Cut a 6x15-inch rectangle of black fabric. Fold in half lengthwise; tuck the raw edges inside at the shirt ends and press. Topstitch along the folded edges.

Attach four grommets on *each* of the short ends. Place vest around doll over blouse; tack in place and lace yarn through grommets at front.

**Skirt:** Sew short ends of striped fabric together, with right sides facing (center back seam).

Hem one long edge; run a gathering thread through the other edge. Put the skirt on the doll, and gather the waist to fit. Tuck under the raw edge; sew the skirt to the vest.

Tie the apron on the doll and tack her hands to her face.

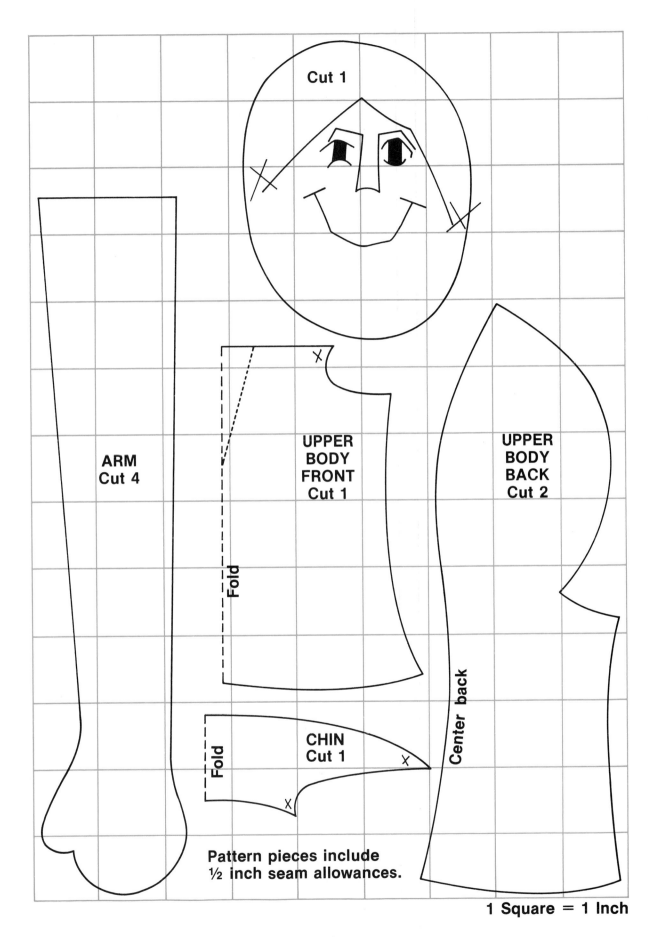

Cut 1

ARM
Cut 4

UPPER
BODY
FRONT
Cut 1

Fold

UPPER
BODY
BACK
Cut 2

Center back

Fold

CHIN
Cut 1

Pattern pieces include
½ inch seam allowances.

1 Square = 1 Inch

# P·I·N·C·U·S·H·I·O·N   P·E·D·D·L·E·R

## TO WHITTLE AND STITCH

Inspired by the carved wooden playthings of pioneer days, this unusual pincushion doll stands just 8 inches tall. If you're a woodcarver—or have an accomplished whittler in your family—you'll find this doll to be a rewarding challenge to make and a joy to own or give to a favorite friend.

## Materials
- 1¼ x 1½ x 3¾-inch piece of pine
- Two 1¼-inch pieces of ¼-inch dowel (upper arms)
- Two 1¾-inch pieces of ¼-inch dowel (lower arms)
- 1 round toothpick for pegging the arms
- Two ½-inch (No. 2) roundhead brass screws
- Graph paper; sandpaper
- Paint; paintbrushes
- Whittling knife; satin varnish
- ⅓ yard of red plaid fabric (dress)
- Handkerchief (apron)
- Polyester fiberfill
- Notions for peddler's box
- Scraps of lace trim

## Instructions
**Body:** Enlarge patterns for front and side of doll to pine block; drill holes ½ inch deep at shoulders, using 1/16-inch drill bit.

With jigsaw, cut away excess wood on front. Keep cuts outside pattern lines. Before cutting curves, make straight cuts from edge of block to pattern line at neck and waist.

Redraw pattern on side of block. Cut away excess wood, cutting nose and chin area last. Follow solid lines for cutting nose and chin with saw.

**Face:** *Note:* See pattern front view for nose position. Lines are wider than necessary; as you shape the face, carve and sand away excess.

With whittling knife, make a slice cut on the nose lines. These are stop lines—to protect nose from accidental chipping as rest of face is carved.

Use knife to round corners and edges; work from high to low places, turning doll often. When front of head has been rounded somewhat, remove excess wood on the cheeks up to the nose stop lines.

Using the front carving view as a guide, make two short stop lines at center of eyes and make shallow grooves above and below each line.

Use both the front carving view and the dashed lines on the side view to make a stop line cut at the hairline; begin shaping hair.

Shaded areas on front carving view show whittling to form cheeks and slight hump between the nose and chin. As you remove small chips in shaded areas, turn the doll, looking from all angles to keep the face from becoming lopsided.

Blend bridge of nose into forehead and corners of eyes.

Slightly curve the eye stop line to form eyelid; make a second very shallow curved cut above each eyelid.

Carefully shape the nose, flaring the nostrils (see painting view). Carve small nostrils.

Form mouth about ⅓ of the way from the nostrils to the chin. Mark with a pencil. Make shallow stop line cut with the knife.

With the tip of the knife remove two small chips at each side of the center upper lip and one chip at the center of the lower lip. The stop line will be slightly longer than these chips.

Whittle any additional refinements necessary to give the doll a pleasant, well-balanced look. Then sand and varnish the head and body.

**Arms:** Cut a ¼-inch-deep mortise in the upper arms. Shape the hands on lower arms; whittle tenons as shown. Reverse shaping for right arm.

Join upper and lower arm. The tenons must fit *perfectly* into the mortise. When properly fitted, hold the pieces snugly with fingers or a vise so they can't move. Drill 1/16-inch hole through both pieces. Insert a round toothpick into the hole. Trim ends.

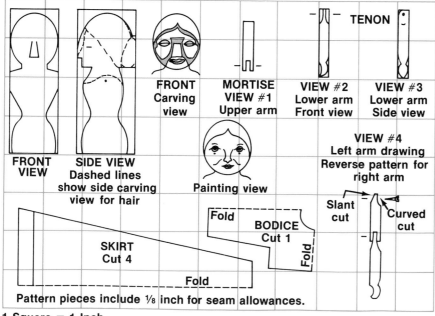

FRONT VIEW

SIDE VIEW Dashed lines show side carving view for hair

FRONT Carving view

Painting view

MORTISE VIEW #1 Upper arm

VIEW #2 Lower arm Front view

VIEW #3 Lower arm Side view

TENON

VIEW #4 Left arm drawing Reverse pattern for right arm

Slant cut

Curved cut

SKIRT Cut 4

Fold

BODICE Cut 1

Fold

Fold

Pattern pieces include ⅛ inch for seam allowances.

1 Square = 1 Inch

In order for arms to bend toward the center front of the doll, the slant and curved cuts at top of arm must be made on a slight angle from mortise and tenon joint at elbow (see views 4, 5, 6). To decide correct placement for slant cut, hold arm alongside doll shoulder; slightly rotate the arm while checking direction of arm bend. Mark placement of slant cut with pencil. Make slant cut and curved cut; drill hole with ³⁄₃₂-inch bit (view 4).

Sand arms smooth. Varnish body and arms; sand again.

Paint face and hair. After paint is dry, varnish.

**Clothing:** Enlarge the patterns onto graph paper; cut out. Patterns include ⅛ inch for seam allowances, unless noted, *below.* Cut bodice front, back, and skirt from plaid fabric.

**Bodice:** Cut center back open; seal raw edges with narrow bead of white glue applied with a toothpick. Trim neckline and sleeves with narrow lace. Sew underarm seams (¼-inch seam); clip corners and turn.

**Skirt:** Sew seams, leaving 1 inch open from the waist on the center back seam. Gather waist to fit bodice. Fit dress onto doll; slip-stitch back seam. Sew on buttons (small beads).

**Doll base:** Cut one 8½-inch-diameter circle from cardboard. Cut a second circle from fabric, adding ½ inch for seam allowance. Gather edge of fabric; pull snug around cardboard. Turn up skirt hem ½ inch. Stuff the skirt with fiberfill; whipstitch the base to the opening.

**Apron:** Fashion apron from hankie; sew to waist.

**Peddler's tray:** Make a 1x1½ inch tray (about ½ inch high) from pine; pad the center (to hold needles and pins) and cover with red polka-dot fabric. Trim with lace. Drill holes in sides for attaching sewing notions.

Add purchased miniature sewing notions to tray. Or, make button cards from oaktag and use small seed beads or pearls for buttons. Whittle tiny spools of thread from excess wood; cover with thread. Cut yardstick from wood. Wrap baby rickrack or narrow, delicate lace around oaktag. Hang the notions from the tray using sturdy thread.

# J·U·M·P·I·N·G   J·A·C·K

**C**hildren of all ages will laugh along with our sprightly marionette. Designed to resemble court jesters of yesteryear, this perky fellow has limbs that swing freely. When you pull the strings, he jumps to delight young and old alike, just as he might have for a king's command performance. Display the doll on a bedroom wall and he'll capture a tot's or teen's fancy, too.

## Materials
- ½ yard of unbleached muslin
- 1 yard of satin fabric (suit)
- ¼ yard of velvet (hat)
- ¼ yard of satin (hat lining)
- Roll of quilt batting
- 7 yards of rattail nylon cord
- Carpet thread; white glue
- Buttons (eyes and suit)
- Feathers and ornaments for hat
- Red felt scrap
- Powdered rouge
- ½-inch dowel; ice pick
- Large wooden bead
- 1 skein of brown yarn (hair)

## Instructions
Finished size is 38 inches.

Enlarge patterns, *opposite,* onto brown paper, adding ¼-inch seam allowances.

**Head:** Cut face and head shapes from muslin. Using two layers of muslin for each pattern piece, pin, baste, and sew layers together, right sides facing. Stitch face sections together; stitch head back to face front, leaving opening for turning. Turn and stuff *very firmly.* Insert cardboard at back of head to stiffen. Turn raw edges under; slip-stitch opening closed.

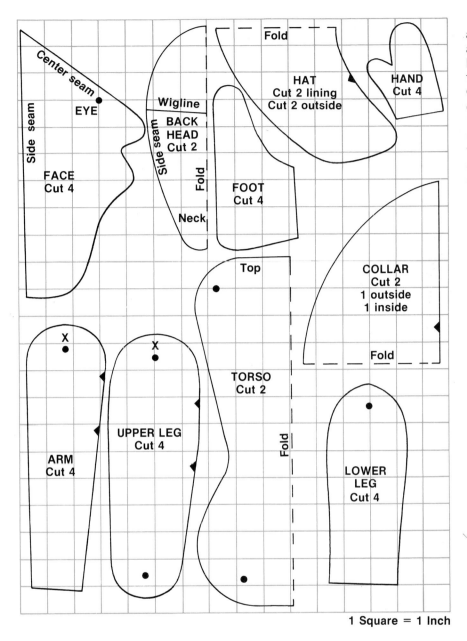

**1 Square = 1 Inch**

To assemble arms, stitch hands to arms at wrist line. With right sides of arms facing, stitch arm/hand assemblies together, leaving seam open between dots. *Do not turn to right side.* Cut two layers of batting and one layer of muslin the same size as the arm. Pin and baste these extra layers, with muslin layer on top, to one of the wrong-side pattern pieces. Trim the seams to ⅛ inch and turn, making sure that the correct layer ends right side up. Slip-stitch opening closed.

Complete torso, upper legs, and lower legs in the same manner, stitching shoes to lower legs before assembling. Make collar as for hat. Gather collar with running stitches; pull taut until gathered edge fits the front of the suit between side seams of suit. Secure collar. Stitch buttons to suit.

**To assemble jumping jack:** Push the ice pick through the jump string dot on the left shoulder and through the dot on the left arm. Cut fourteen 6-inch pieces of black rattail cord, applying white glue to the ends to stiffen and prevent fraying. When the glue is dry, force two strands of cord through the hole in the shoulder and then through the hole in the arm using the ice pick as your pusher. Tie ends of both cords together at the back of the arm to form a large knot. Pull up the cords in the front as tightly as possible and tie in a knot; trim cord and re-apply glue. Use the same procedure to attach other arm, upper legs at hips, and lower legs at the knee.

**To make the doll jump:** Using the ice pick, insert a 36-inch length of cord into the arm at the hinge string dot—*do not insert it through the shoulder.* Tie the end of the cord in a large knot on the back of the arm; trim end. Repeat for other arm. Insert a 24-inch length of cord into the upper leg at the hinge string dot—*do not insert it through the lower leg.* Knot as instructed above. Repeat for remaining leg. Thread all four cords through a large macrame bead and knot them together at heel level. Place remaining 6-inch pieces of cord side by side and knot into a double-strand loop. Sew knot to center back of head. Hold jumping jack by loop; pull down on bead to make jack jump.

**Hair:** Cut a 3x10-inch wig strip pattern from cardboard. Wind the yarn around the width of the cardboard until yarn covers 5 inches of the cardboard length. Cut yarn off to get 6-inch yarn strands. Cut *muslin* wig strip; center yarn strands along the length. Machine-stitch yarn to strip, sewing down the center. Trim muslin to ½ inch wide; fold muslin strip in half (for double hair thickness), and tack wig in place along wig line of head.

**Hat:** Trace hat pattern onto hat and lining fabric. Stitch velvet hat pieces together with right sides facing, but leave area between dots open for turning. Turn to right side. Repeat for lining, *except* do not turn lining to right side. With wrong sides facing, insert lining inside hat. Slip-stitch lining to hat. Stitch feather and ornament in place; tack hat to head.

To complete face, sew button eyes and red felt mouth in place. Brush cheeks with powdered rouge.

**Body:** Cut out hands and lower legs from muslin. Cut torso, upper legs, arms, and collar from suit fabric. Cut shoes from velvet.

# P·A·J·A·M·A·B·A·G   P·A·L

**L**ike a fairy tale character come to life, this pajama-bag doll will befriend your child and you, too. For your youngster, he's a life-size playmate in a colorful peasant costume (including a leather pouch for special treasures). For you, he's a helper with trousers roomy enough to keep pajamas off the bedroom floor.

## Materials

Yardage is for 44-inch-wide fabric.
- 1 yard of muslin (body)
- 1 yard of woven tan fabric (shirt)
- ½ yard *each* of red wool (boots) and red cotton (legs, dickey)
- ½ yard of 50-inch-wide striped brown wool (pants)
- 14-inch-square of red felt (hat)
- Scraps of gray suede (pouch)
- Polyester fiberfill
- ¼ skein of brown yarn (hair)
- 1 yard of ½-inch-wide leather strapping (belt); two feathers
- ¾ yard of ½-inch-wide elastic
- Gray and black embroidery floss
- Black yarn (ties and lacings)

## Instructions

The doll is 36 inches tall.

Enlarge pattern, *left,* onto paper; cut out. Cut paper rectangles measuring 14½x19 inches (sleeves), 5x10½ inches (pant cuffs), and 5x8 inches (dickey). All patterns include ½-inch seam allowances.

**Body:** Cut back, front, chin, and arms from muslin. Cut legs from red cotton-blend fabric.

Place muslin over face pattern; trace lines on muslin with quiltmaker's transfer pen. Outline-stitch face lines and satin-stitch eyes with gray floss. Add black outline stitches under gray upper eyelid lines. Straight-stitch radiating pupil lines and satin-stitch pupils with black. Color lips and cheeks using two shades of pink powdered rouge. Cut out face pattern.

*Note:* Stitch all pieces together with right sides facing.

Sew chin to face between ears. Stitch dart in body front; stitch neck edge of chin to neck of body front.

Stitch center-back seam. Stitch front to back, leaving bottom open. Clip curves, trim, and turn.

Stitch arms and legs together (in pairs), leaving tops open. Clip curves, trim, and turn. Stuff with fiberfill. Sew openings closed; stitch limbs to body.

**Hair:** Cut 5-inch lengths of yarn. (See pattern for hairline and use as a guide for hair length.) Hand-sew clusters of yarn to head front. Sew a few clusters behind ears and back of neck. (Cap hides rest of head.)

**Clothing: For hat:** Cut a 12-inch-diameter circle from *center* of red felt. Using pattern, cut brim from remaining scrap. Gather circle ¼ inch from edge to fit measurement of curved brim edge. Stitch center seam at brim back. Pin gathered circle to brim; sew together ½ inch from raw edges.

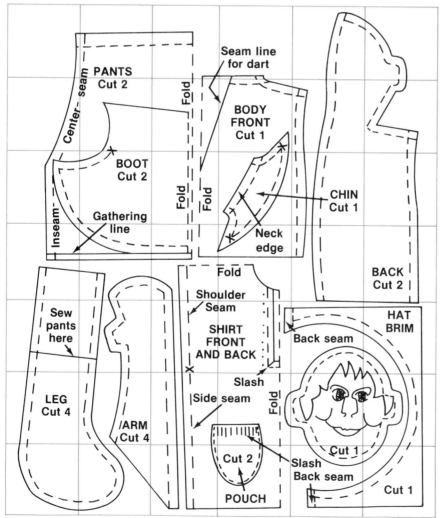

1 Square = 5 Inches

Tuck raw edges inside, place back-brim seam at head back; stitch hat to head. Add feathers.

Cut boots, pants and two cuffs, shirt, shirt sleeves, and dickey from fabrics indicated in materials list.

**Shirt:** Sew the sleeves on shirt at shoulders between Xs. Stitch underarm and side seams. Put shirt on doll; place dickey inside the shirt opening. Fold raw edges of shirt opening to the inside; whipstitch onto doll, fastening dickey inside at same time. Gather neck edge to fit; stitch to doll. To form cuffs, fold under 6 inches at bottom of sleeves. Roll 3 inches back for cuffs; tack at seam line. Thread black yarn on darning needle; sew crisscross lacing on shirt front.

**Pants:** Stitch center front and back seams. Sew gathering stitches at the pants bottoms; stitch inseams. For casing, fold waist edge under ¼ inch, then ¾ inch; sew along the folded edge, leaving an opening for elastic. Insert elastic and stitch the opening closed. Trim seams, clip the curves, and turn.

Place pants on doll; tuck the shirt inside. Gather pants bottoms and slip-stitch gathers to doll's legs (see the pattern). Stitch short ends of pants cuffs together. Fold the pants cuffs in half lengthwise; press. Fold the raw edges under ½ inch; slip-stitch folded edges of cuffs over gathers in pants.

**Boots:** Stitch the bottom and toe seams, ending seams at Xs. Clip curves, trim seams, and turn. Stitch ½-inch hems at tops; fold front openings inside ½ inch; slip-stitch in place. Put boots on doll; secure.

For boot ties, thread darning needle with black yarn and run yarn through boots 1½ inches from tops; pull yarn and tie into bows. Stitch crisscross lacings around legs.

**Pouch:** Cut patterns from suede. Stitch together around curved edge; turn. Slash pouch top, stopping slashes ¾ inch from raw edge. Cut scrap suede into a long ¼-inch-wide strip; thread through slashes; pull strip taut. Tie pouch to belt; knot belt on doll.

Stuff pajamas into back of pants.

# S·A·C·H·E·T    D·O·L·L·S

**W**hat nicer way to gift a bride-to-be than with these elegant, romantic miniatures. To make them, begin with the full-size patterns on pages 78 and 79. Lavishly embellish both figures with paint, embroidery, and beads. Then fill them with rose blossoms and other sweet-scented potpourri.

## Materials

- ⅓ yard of white (or off-white) cotton-blend fabric
- Permanent brown fine-tip marking pen
- Dressmaker's carbon paper
- Tissue paper
- Ecru sewing thread
- The following materials are optional, depending on how you plan to decorate and finish the dolls:
  Embroidery floss
  Embroidery hoop
  Embroidery needle
  Metallic thread
  Fabric paints
  Paintbrushes
  Polyester fiberfill
  Seed pearls, beads, laces, and other trims
  Cardboard for bases
  ⅛-inch-wide ribbon for hanging
  Artist's oil pencils
  Fabric crayons
  Scented potpourri

## Instructions

Trace full-size patterns on pages 78 and 79 onto paper. Using a blunt point (such as a dry pen tip) and dressmaker's carbon, transfer patterns onto fabric. *Leave 1 inch around each doll for seam allowances.* Draw over lines with permanent marker.

**Decorating the dolls:** Keep in mind that you may leave the dolls plain. However, if you choose to decorate them, the dolls should be painted and embroidered before they are cut and stitched.

**Painting the dolls:** Use high-quality acrylic or fabric paints. Place a small amount of paint on a glass plate or palette. Then, thin the paint with a few drops of water until it is the consistency of light cream. To lighten the color of the paint, add a drop of white paint to a few drops of water and mix the white paint with a color. If necessary, add a few more drops of water to further lighten the effect.

To mix two colors of paint, follow the same procedure, *above,* mixing the two colors until you achieve the desired shade.

Place the fabric dolls on several layers of newspaper or paper towels. To begin painting, dip a small brush in paint and remove excess water by lightly dabbing the brush on a paper towel. (Excess water makes the paint bleed on the fabric. Do not place too much paint on the brush at a time.)

Beginning with the large areas first, paint *up to, but not over,* the brown outlines. To prevent the colors from bleeding, allow each painted area to dry before beginning to paint an adjacent area. Use a light wash of color when painting areas so the decorative lines (such as the folds and flowers on the bride's gown) will show through the paint.

When dolls are dry, gently press the wrong side of the fabric with a warm iron. For extra body, add a light coat of spray starch.

To clean brushes, rinse them thoroughly in running water.

**Crayons:** Use high-quality crayons or specially formulated fabric crayons (available at art supply stores). Color the front and back of each doll in the desired colors, being careful not to leave flecks of wax on the fabric.

To set the colors, place the fabric faceup on several layers of clean paper towels and cover the fabric with more paper towels. Press the fabric with a hot iron. Change the paper towels and repeat if necessary.

**Colored pencils:** Use high-quality colored pencils or artist's oil pencils. These pencils yield a wide range of values, depending on the amount of pressure you apply.

After coloring the dolls, press the fabric, following the instructions for the crayon dolls.

**Permanent fine-tip marking pens:** Choose fine-tip marking pens that do not bleed on fabric and that will not cause the brown outlines to bleed. To test your pens, mark on a piece of scrap fabric.

Use light colors since the ink from a marking pen often looks darker when applied to fabric.

To color the dolls, mark each area lightly, being careful not to obliterate the brown outlines.

When finished, press the fabric on the wrong side, using a warm iron.

**Embroidery floss:** Combine just a touch of embroidery with painting if desired, or use embroidery alone to highlight certain details.

Use cotton, silk, metallic, or linen threads, or lightweight pearl cotton for special effects.

Limit embroidery to facial features, hair, clothing details, and flowers, rather than trying for an overall embroidered effect.

*(continued)*

## Sachet Dolls

*(continued)*

Using a single strand of embroidery floss throughout, work the facial features in outline stitches, with French knots and satin stitches for highlights. (Refer to stitch diagrams, *opposite,* and embroidery books for stitch howto.) Work bullion knots, *shown opposite,* in clusters for roses.

To form a bullion knot, work a backstitch the length of the stitch required; bring the needle up through the fabric where the needle first enters the fabric. *Do not pull the thread taut.* Wrap the excess thread around the point of the needle as many times as required to completely fill the space of the backstitch.

Hold your thumb on the coiled thread and pull the threaded needle through the coils. Insert the needle back through point A. Pull the thread until bullion knot lies flat.

For best results, use a needle with a small eye so that the thread passes easily through the coils.

**Beads:** Embellish some of the design motifs with small beads, seed pearls, or glass jewels, if desired. String the beads on a strand of thread and tack the beads in place.

**Quilting:** After all other decorating is completed, the dolls may be trapunto-quilted for added dimension.

Pin muslin, organdy, or other lightweight fabric backing to the wrong side of the fabric doll.

Quilt along the design lines you wish to emphasize—clothing or accessories, for example.

After quilting, use small, sharp scissors to carefully cut a slit in the *backing fabric only.* Place a small piece of stuffing between the two layers of fabric and whipstitch slit edges together.

**Full size bride and groom**

**Assembly:** Cut out the decorated fronts and plain backs for each doll, leaving at least ⅝ inch of fabric around the solid outlines (this allows ⅛-inch seam allowances). With right sides facing, pin and baste front and back sides together, matching solid outlines carefully.

Sew dolls together by hand or machine, stitching ⅛ inch outside solid outlines, and following the curves as closely as possible. Leave an opening in each doll for turning and stuffing. Or, leave bottom edge of doll open and cut a fabric oval for the base of each doll. For stability, line

each fabric oval with a piece of cardboard. Trim seams and clip curves.

Turn each doll right-side out, making sure each curve and corner is turned to the stitching line.

Stuff the dolls with small pieces of polyester fiberfill, beginning at the head and gradually working your way down. Do not overstuff and do not leave gaps between pieces of fiberfill.

Slip-stitch openings closed, turning raw edges under. Or, stitch each fabric base in place, inserting cardboard ovals for lining.

For scented sachets, fill each doll with potpourri instead of fiberfill. To make a potpourri, clip rose petals during the summer and dry them in a shady, well-ventilated place. Store petals in an airtight container for several weeks, stirring every few days. Add a mixture of lavender, orrisroot, tonka bean, sandalwood, lemon verbena, frankincense, and myrrh; cure, covered, for about six weeks, stirring the mixture frequently.

Use nylon thread or narrow ribbon loops to hang the dolls, if desired.

## Basic Embroidery Stitches

Included here are diagrams for the embroidery stitches most often mentioned in this book. Particular stitches are noted in the how-to instructions for the dolls. But don't be afraid to experiment with new stitches that you think would be appropriate for faces, hair, and clothing details.

Backstitch

Buttonhole stitch

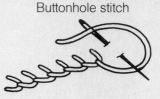

Bullion stitch

Chain stitch

French-knot stitch

Long-and-short stitch

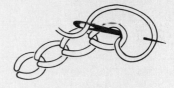

Outline stitch
(also called stem stitch)

Satin stitch

Straight stitch

Turkey-work stitch

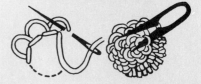

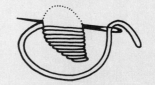

# CREDITS

**Designers**
We wish to express our appreciation and sincere thanks to everyone who contributed designs to this book.

Taresia Boernke, 15, 32-33, 41, 56
Judy Brown, 71
Sue Bruni, 20-21, 38
Coats & Clark, 59
Phyllis Dunstan, 44, 64-65
Mary Engelbreit, 8, 15, 63
Dorothy and John Everds, 11, 54
Bobbi Jo Free, 28
Laura Holtorf, 8
Rebecca Jerdee, 67, 75
Jude Martin, 50-51
Janet McCaffery, 4, 76
Susan Morrison, 27
Robin Rice, 24
Terry Ryder, 72
Mimi Shimmin, 46-47, 60
Ciba Vaughan, 4, 43

**Photographers**
Our thanks also go to these people whose creative talents and technical skills were a valuable help to us in producing this book.

Mike Dieter, 56, 64-65
Jim Hedrich for Hedrich-Blessing, 43
William N. Hopkins and Associates,
    Cover, 14-15, 20-21, 24, 28, 38, 41,
    44, 50-51, 54, 59, 60, 67, 71, 72, 76
Scott Little, 4-5, 8, 11, 46-47, 63
Perry Struse, 27, 32-33, 75

Have BETTER HOMES AND GARDENS® magazine delivered to your door. For information, write MR. ROBERT AUSTIN, P.O. BOX 4536, DES MOINES, IA 50336.